1984 GREEN COIN BOOK

THIRTEENTH EDITION

A complete, illustrated catalog of U.S. coins
and bills and their cash premium values
from 1652 to the present
and
The complete coinage of Canada and Newfoundland
from 1858 to date

BY ROBERT FRIEDBERG
EDITED BY ARTHUR L. AND IRA S. FRIEDBERG

Associate editor: Arthur S. Goldenberg
Contributing editors: Gus Goldi and Jack M. Molnar

Bell Publishing Company
New York

CONTENTS

A Note from the Publishers

The cash premium values in this book are published for the information and guidance of all concerned—for those who have coins for sale as well as for those who want a complete reference work on the market value of coins and currency.

The valuations listed do not indicate retail prices, but instead, closely approximate how much established coin dealers will actually pay for any material needed in their stock. The valuations are based on the coins being in Good to Very Good condition, unless otherwise noted. Coins in better condition are worth more.

The editors are professional coin dealers. Anyone interested in either buying or selling coins and paper money may contact them at the following address: The Coin & Currency Institute, Inc., 102 Linwood Plaza, Fort Lee, NJ 07024. When shipping coins, be sure to use insured or registered mail.

Since silver has risen to its current levels, many coins are being traded solely for their silver value. Most coin dealers are paying a premium over face value for any and all of these silver coins regardless of date or condition; in many cases, even uncirculated coins are not worth more than their melt value. For the purposes of this book, silver has been calculated at $13.50 per ounce. Therefore, all dimes, quarters and half-dollars which are valued at $1.00, $2.50 and $5.00 respectively, fluctuate in relation to the commodity price of silver and the actual premium value will vary accordingly.

Because of this, the cash premium values of Silver coins, dollars, Commemorative Half Dollars, Proof Sets and gold coins are subject to fluctuation.

Do not clean or polish any coins! They will lose a great deal of their premium value if you do. Coins should be left in the same condition as when found, no matter how dark they may appear.

Preface

At some time or another almost all of us acquire or come across some coins or old pieces of paper money which excite our curiosity or otherwise hold our interest. What is it about these coins that has thus captured our attention? It may have been the strangeness of denomination (a copper 2 Cent piece or a nickel 3 Cent piece or a silver Half Dime or a 3 Dollar gold piece); it may have been antiquity (a large Cent of 1794 or a Colonial Copper of 1694); or the surprise of discovering for yourself an untoward bit of information (that we once used a 15 Cent piece of paper money that was, and still is, legal tender); it may have been sheer, compelling intrinsic value (any gold coin) or immediate negotiable value (an old large size 5 Dollar bill); or it may have been the historical associations evoked by the coins (the Battle of Gettysburg, the exploits of Daniel Boone, the Landing of the Pilgrims, the discovery of America itself); or perhaps it was the glittering beauty of perfection (a set of current coins in brilliant proof condition, or a single older coin so finely preserved that it assumed the status of a gem in your mind).

No matter which quality it has been, or what circumstance introduced you to the coins, you have held them in your hand, you have scrutinized them (perhaps under a magnifying glass), you have conjured with them in your imagination, and after the first flush of recognition has passed and the pride of ownership has asserted itself, one question, one unknown factor still remains unanswered for you—how much are these coins worth? It is at this point that for you

THE SEARCH FOR RARE COINS

has begun, a pursuit, or pastime, if you will, indulged in passionately by millions of us for pleasure or for profit. That your coins are worth more than their face value, there is somehow no doubt in your mind. You have been conditioned to believe it, or at the least, to hope it, by the larger and larger amounts of rare coin publicity in recent years.

A boy, rummaging around among his grandmother's effects, finds an 1856 Flying Eagle Cent and sells it to a coin dealer for several hundred dollars; the story is picked up by a news association and is carried in the daily press from coast to coast—or the Treasury Department throws into circulation through the banking system several million silver dollars (as it did in the mid-1960's)—coins which had lain in the vaults for a generation, undisturbed, still in bright, newly minted condition and containing many dates considered rare. The story is headlined in a great eastern daily and almost at once the switchboard of a leading coin dealer is clogged with thousands of incoming phone calls—urgent inquiries from both buyers and sellers—or a banker leaves a map with his will, leading to a hoard of gold coins buried on his estate. The government seizes the coins, you read about it, you hear about it, and you wait to see if the heirs will ever get the coins. The story has a happy ending; they do. The government says that all gold coins may be freely bought and sold or otherwise traded in.

On the other hand, you may have heard some tales about coins that are not quite authentic. You cannot find a 1913 Liberty Head Nickel, because only five pieces were minted and all are accounted for in known collections; and the likelihood of finding an 1804 Silver Dollar or a 5 Dollar gold piece of 1822, or a Brasher Doubloon challenges the laws of probability; no U.S. coin has ever been called in because of a defect in the design; the Columbian Half Dollar of 1892 is *not* worth $10,000.00, as was once mistakenly reported.

The so-called fabulous coins do, of course, exist, but they are not easily to be found or had. The great rarities of U.S. coinage—the pieces that bring many hundreds of dollars—were recognized as rare and valuable almost immediately after striking and they have been jealously guarded ever since by the intelligent, well-informed and alert collectors in each generation. Therefore, if one does come across an 1827 Quarter, or an 1838-O Half-Dollar, or an 1804 Silver Dollar; if you should have a 3 Dollar gold piece of 1875 or a 4 Dollar gold piece of 1880 or a 5 Dollar gold piece of 1815, then it is most likely that these coins were originally purchased as rare collectors items for large sums of money, and have come from a highly regarded coin collection, rather than from the accumulated small change of bygone days.

But instead of a few dozen legendary pieces, we still have the main output of U.S. coinage for our field of activity, containing, as it does, multitudes of coins with cash premium values ranging from the modest to the substantial. It is the search for, and the recognition of these coins that is occupying so many millions of Americans today, for pleasure as a pastime or for business as a profession. It is for them and for you that this volume has been created, and in our attempt to make it the finest and most useful coin book of its kind in existence it has of necessity become

A COMPLETE CATALOGUE OF U.S. COINS

from 1652 to date, including the pre-revolutionary Colonial coinage as well as the Pioneer gold coinage struck after the California gold rush at the various Territorial Mints.

We have thus accounted for all the "hard money" that has ever been issued in this country; but what of our paper money? The first U.S. Government notes were issued in 1861 and since then many rare and valuable notes have been produced, including some of quite recent years. These are just as much sought after and collected as are coins and for many years now currency for collectors has assumed an importance equal to that of coins.

We have therefore decided to present the subject of American monetary issues in its entirety and accordingly you will find in this book, as an adjunct to the coin listing, a companion catalogue of

ALL TYPES AND SERIES OF U.S. PAPER MONEY
ALL TYPES OF CONFEDERATE PAPER MONEY

from 1861 to the present day and including (a) the early large size notes, (b) the later or present size notes, (c) Fractional Currency issues—the 3, 5, 10, 15, 25 and 50 Cent notes which circulated as U.S. paper money in the 1860's and 1870's, and which are still legal tender, (d) Confederate Paper Money from the 50 Cent note to the 1000 Dollar note.

The tabular arrangement used in cataloguing the paper money has been designed for efficient use and the information given is both concise and complete, so that even without illustrations, you will be able to locate and identify any note without any confusion.

The concluding section of this book is devoted to the coinage of our neighbors to the north, with whom we share such a long common border. As with the U.S. coinage, we have aimed for thorough coverage and in these pages you will also find a complete catalogue of

THE COINS OF CANADA AND NEWFOUNDLAND

together with those of New Brunswick, Nova Scotia, Prince Edward Island and British Columbia. The Canadian series begins in 1858 when the first, true coins on the Dollar or Decimal standard were issued.

The inclusion of the Canadian series in this catalogue is not an afterthought but is rather dictated by the existing necessity for this information, since the Canadian issues rank next in popularity to U.S. coins. Canadian coins are now considered as important as our domestic coins, and in some sections of the country they form the major part of numismatic activity. A glance at the catalogue will reveal many coins with high premium values and an active interest in the coinage of British North America can prove to be a rewarding experience.

With the inclusion of the Canadian series in this volume the publishers believe this to be

A UNIQUE BOOK

in the annals of numismatic literature, since never before has so much varied and useful information been offered in a single, low-priced, convenient book. For example, until now there has never been a listing in the same book of the premium values of paper money together with coins. The premium books of the past have rarely had listings with any completeness of both Colonial coins and Pioneer gold coins.

It is thus believed that by the proper reference to this book, one should be able to evaluate any coin of American origin, any type of U.S. or Confederate paper money and any coin in the British North American series.

It is important at this point to attempt an answer to the question

WHAT MAKES A COIN VALUABLE?

a perplexing and sometimes vexing question. At the outset let it be said that mere age alone has nothing to do with establishing the value of a coin. Many persons mistakenly regard the figure 100 with especial reverence, thinking that the age of 100 years or more automatically confers a special value on a coin. This is simply not so, as an analysis of the coin valuations will reveal. For example, the 1794 Cent commands a premium of $30.00, but the 1914-D Cent brings

$50.00. A bronze coin of ancient Greece from about 350 B.C. can be bought for about $20.00; a silver coin of Rome from about 200 A.D. for about $40.00; an English Shilling of Queen Elizabeth dated 1587 for about $25.00—and so on—yet a *1932-D Quarter—only 49 years old at the present writing has a premium value of $35.00.*

There are actually three factors which combine to determine the cash premium value of any coin, namely, rarity, demand and condition. The first of these

RARITY

is the most important, since without rarity, the other two factors are only of minor significance. A coin becomes rare out of various circumstances; it may be struck in much fewer numbers than is normal for a contemporary coin of that type (witness the 1877 Cent, the 1931-S Cent, the 1885 Nickel, the 1916-D Dime, the 1901-S Quarter); or it may be a coin of a type struck in only one year (witness the 1793 Half-Cent, the 1796 Quarter, the 1808 Quarter Eagle, the 1907 Double Eagle with Roman numerals); or it may be a coin struck in relatively large numbers for the period but of which only a very few have survived (witness the 1802 Half-Dime, the 1873-CC Dime, the 1876-CC 20 Cent piece, the 1822 Half-Eagle); or it may be one of the fabled pieces of which so few were struck to begin with that it became a great rarity on the day of minting (witness the 1913 Liberty Head Nickel, the 1894-S Dime, the 1804 Silver dollar, the 1885 Trade dollar, any proof coin before 1858); or, as is also likely, the rarity may be determined by the condition of the coin. In these days when millions of collectors are competing for and buying up the choicest specimens, coins which may be very common in used or circulated condition have become quite rare in new or uncirculated condition (witness the entire series of 10, 25 and 50 cent pieces from 1892 to 1933, all Liberty Head nickels, most Indian Head cents, early Lincoln cents with mint marks, etc.). In fact almost any uncirculated coin before about 1930 is now considered scarce in one degree or another.

Assuming then that a given coin is of some rarity, another factor that determines its value is

DEMAND

which is both judge and jury and your only true indicator of the coin's popularity in the numismatic market place. No matter how rare a coin may be, it cannot be easily sold for a price commensurate with its rarity, unless there is a demand for it by collectors. This demand manifests itself to the professional coin dealer through his customers. Repeated requests for a coin not in his stock automatically create a demand for that coin, and if he wishes to stay in business, he must sooner or later buy it. The ultimate demand is thus created by the ultimate consumer, the collector himself, but the large amounts of cash that support the numismatic market are furnished by the professional coin dealers, who thus perform an essential service for both seller and buyer.

It is obvious that all coins cannot be equally in demand at all times; that is why so many coins appear to have a value disproportionately high or low in relation to their rarity. As mentioned above, demand, and hence value, is created by the mass of collectors who are subject to all sorts of collecting impulses. Hence there are fashions, changes of taste and recurrent cycles in coin collecting, as there are in other cultural pursuits. One year Roosevelt Dimes may be the rage; the next year Franklin Half-Dollars; then it may be Proof Sets or Commemoratives or rolls of coins.

But out of all the welter of intense numismatic activity, one trend remains constant through the years—the lower the denomination of the coin, the greater the demand. Hence the King of American coins is the Cent. There are millions more who collect cents—Lincoln and Indian—than any other coins; many more who collect dimes than quarters; many more who collect silver dollars than 5 dollar gold pieces; and many more who collect 20 dollar gold pieces than 50 Dollar bills.

One example selected out of many will show how demand is uncompromising and inexorable in determining coin values. The 1914-D Lincoln cent with a coinage of 1,193,000 pieces has a listed premium value of $50.00; but the 1914-S Quarter with a much smaller coinage of 264,000 pieces lists at only $7.00; compare both with the Cent of 1814—a hundred years earlier—which has a coinage of 357,800 pieces and a listed value of $15.00. Obviously, the 1914-D Cent will tend to keep increasing in value, whereas the other two coins will tend to remain about as they are—unless there is a radical change in collecting habits.

An analysis of the material in this book will reveal much interesting and some surprising data about our coins and their values. Fortunately for numismatics, there are now so many collectors clamoring for all types of coins and there is so much nationwide interest in coin and currency collecting, that one will find a ready sale for almost any American coin, providing always, of course, that it is in suitable

CONDITION

for collecting purposes, since condition, or the state of preservation, is the third factor that helps determine the value of a coin.

Regarded purely as objects of the past (a Greek urn, a Flemish tapestry, a Colt firearm), coins are desired by collectors in the finest condition in which they can be found, within a given price range. Some can afford the finest pieces, others only the average ones. Perhaps this love of new, beautiful coins goes back to our childhood. How pleased we were to be given a new, shiny coin in our change and how reluctant we were to spend it! The true collector among us did not spend it but put it away—if he could afford it—and when found again many years later, it would still be in new condition and by then it would have gained something else—numismatic value.

In this respect a new coin can be likened to a beautiful woman in the full bloom of her youth—lustrous, desirable and admired by all; but as she circulates through the days and years of her life, subtle changes occur in her appearance and after a certain length of time she bears little resemblance to the thing she once was; only her identity is the same; but if only she were the Sleeping Beauty of the fable, she would be found one hundred years later, still lustrous, desirable and admired by all. Coins have become the true sleeping beauties of our generation and there are many such waiting to be restored to life by the diligent prince charmings who will discover them in their "piggy" banks, attics, family souvenirs, bank vaults, or among long-forgotten, unused possessions.

The condition of a very rare coin is not so important a factor in value as it is of a more common coin. The rare piece would be valuable in its own right and the difference in value between the best and poorest condition would not be too great. Some series of coins tend to exist in choice condition, others in poor condition. For example, most gold coins exist in well preserved, brilliant condition and there is not much difference in value between an average used piece and a new one. (From about $2,000.00 to $10,000.00 for the 5 Dollar gold piece of 1795.) Early Large Cents, on the other hand, exist mostly in quite worn condition and new pieces are very rare indeed (from about $25.00 to $1,000.00 for the Large Cent of 1795). Among the more modern coins for example the 1927-S Quarter in average used condition has a premium listing of only $7.00 but a new or uncirculated specimen can easily be sold for $ 1500.00 because it is so very rare in this choice condition. Similarly, from used to new, the 1926-S Nickel ranges from $2.75 to about $400.00, the 1921 Half-Dollar from $35.00 to about $2,000.00; the 1927-D Dime from $ 1.00 to about $250.00. But the 1909-S-VDB Cent, which is a rare coin in any condition, has a narrow range of values, and a used piece brings about $ 200.00, a new piece about $350.00.

It is thus evident that condition is intimately tied to rarity and hence to demand, and it is these three factors operating together in various proportions that determine the price at which a coin can be sold at a given time in a given place.

The condition of a coin is usually denoted by a degree of fineness. (Please note that the numismatic meaning of the word "fine" is quite different from its literary meaning, as will be seen below.) The standard terms used in grading the condition of coins, their abbreviations, and what the terms mean are as follows:—

PROOF or PR. The ultimate condition of coins, since proof coins are struck purely for collectors and not for circulation. The greatest care is lavished in their production so that they will emerge as supreme examples of the art of coinage. A premium over face value has always been charged by the Mint for its proof coins. The coins are struck from scientifically polished dies and metal blanks, and the resultant proof coins are easily recognized by their unusual brilliance. They shine like no other coins you have ever seen, because the surface of a proof coin is like that of a spotless mirror. You can actually see yourself in one of these coins.

UNCIRCULATED or UNC. This denotes a coin in new or unused condition and Unc. coins are usually in the same brilliant condition as when they left the mint. That shiny coin you sometimes get from your bank is considered an Unc. coin if you are the first person to whom this coin has been paid out in the normal course of coin distribution from government mint to local bank via the Federal Reserve System. As soon as you have put your finger marks on the coin and let it jingle in your pocket with other coins for any length of time, it is no longer considered Unc. in the true sense of the word.

EXTREMELY FINE or EF. This denotes a coin which has been in circulation so little, that it shows only the slightest sign of wear or use. For the most part, an EF coin still retains the lustre or mint bloom of an Unc. piece. Actually many EF coins are truly Unc. pieces which have been poorly handled through the years, so that they now show slight friction, minor abrasions or other unimportant blemishes.

VERY FINE or VF. A coin described as VF will generally have been in circulation a relatively short time. It will certainly show evidence of use such as loss of lustre, wear on the highest struck portions, and a proportionate amount of small surface markings which, however, do not detract from the over-all choiceness of true VF quality. Every detail of lettering and design that was originally impressed into the coin will be boldly visible. In general, a coin taken out of your change at random, that is from one to two years old, will tend to be in VF condition.

FINE or F. A fine coin has begun to show signs of more obvious circulation and can best be recognized by the letters and numerals appearing on it. By now they have become somewhat thick and blurry from the constant soft friction of circulation. All of the larger letters will be fully visible but the smaller ones may have begun to fade in a coin rated as fine. If the coin is silver, the reeding or milling on the edge will have begun to lose its character, and is approaching the point when it will vanish from the coin altogether, leaving it with a smooth edge. A truly fine coin makes an overall pleasing impression on the eye, as the amount of circulation is nicely and evenly distributed over its entire surface, but is still not severe enough to give the coin a shopworn appearance.

VERY GOOD and GOOD or VG and G. These two terms are all-embracing in scope because they accurately describe the condition of most of the millions of non-current coins now in existence. (By non-current we mean all types of coins except those presently being struck). These terms are used singly as VG and G or sometimes together as G-VG. Coins in either of these two conditions (between which there is only a minor difference in value) are the general, run-of-the-mill, circulated coins found everywhere. They have spent long, faithful years in the service of their country and they look it. The reason so very many of our older type coins are found in this condition is that there were few coin collectors in the old days. Consequently most coins got into circulation and stayed there for many years, passing routinely into the government melting pot or casually into a private holding.

G and VG coins present a well-worn appearance and are in a more advanced state of circulation than fine coins. Most of the larger letters will have shrunk somewhat from the creeping paralysis of circulation, moving from the outer edge of the coin to the center. The smaller lettering may have disappeared altogether, such as the word "Liberty" which appears on the head band of a Liberty-head coin or on an Indian Head Cent. But such coins are still recognizable for what they are; you can easily read the date, the denomination, the main legends and the mint mark, if any. Just as they are the most common, so are they the most widely collected, because they represent decent, collectible coins at moderate prices, the appeal thus being to the great mass of collectors.

In this book, for example, the valuations are based on the coins being in G-VG condition, except as noted elsewhere in the catalogue proper.

FAIR and POOR. These two terms (no standard abbreviations) are used for coins in the lowest possible condition. Such coins are so badly worn or have such defects, that they are barely recognizable and hence are called "space fillers." They will do in a collection simply because better ones cannot be found or may cost too much. Only very rare coins would command a premium in fair or good condition. Such coins might be a 1793 Half-Cent or Cent, a 1794 Dollar, or 1796 Half-Cent, Quarter, or Half-Dollar, etc. Fair and poor coins present an appearance which some have described as miserable. Most of the design and lettering are gone and so little remains on the coin that sometimes only experienced numismatic deduction can properly attribute it.

Sometimes coins will be found that cannot properly be described by any of the above conditions because they have been mutilated in various ways or are false. **Such coins are of no numismatic value and command no premium.** If genuine, they are worth only their face amount, but if a hole has been drilled into any coin it has lost even its face value, since the government will not redeem such a coin. Some of these various mutilations, defects or deceptions are described as follows:—

HOLED. A coin with a hole drilled completely through it.

PLUGGED HOLE. A holed coin in which the hole has been filled in with some metal to reduce the ugliness of the coin.

LOOPED. A coin with a loop attached to the edge by solder, enabling it to be attached to a chain. This is most common in gold coins.

LOOP REMOVED. A coin from which a loop has been removed by breaking or sawing it off. The edge of the coin will usually reveal evidence of a former loop.

GILDED. Any coin which has been gold plated.

NAMES and INITIALS. These will sometimes be found scratched, engraved or stamped on coins. Only in the case of a great rarity would a coin thus mutilated command a premium.

ELECTROTYPE. A false coin made by making impressions of a genuine coin on a thin shell of the same metal. The Obv. and Rev. are on different shells, which are then joined after filling them with a cheap alloy to give them weight. A thin line running around the edge will usually identify an electrotype, as well as the fact that it will not have the true ring of a genuine coin.

CAST. A false coin made by making a cast from a genuine coin. Casts can generally be identified by a rough, mottled surface.

ALTERED DATE. A false coin made by changing the date on a genuine coin to another date of much greater rarity and value. Some altered date coins are very difficult to detect and hence dangerous, bearing in mind that the coin itself is genuine. A strong magnifier will generally discover this deception.

MINT MARK ADDED OR REMOVED. Similar in principle to altered date coins, but in this case, the mint mark, not the date, has been tampered with. A mint mark may be added to a coin or removed from it, in order to make it more valuable. As with altered date coins, a strong magnifier should be used on a suspected piece.

POLISHED COINS. Although not mutilated, coins which have been polished to a high shine by cleaning powders, polishing creams, or other abrasives lose a great deal of their premium value, even if in otherwise choice condition. Coins should be left in the same state of preservation as when found, and no attempt should be made to clean or polish them, no matter how dirty they may appear.

TOKENS—CALIFORNIA GOLD PIECES

Sometimes copper or nickel pieces will be found which appear to be U.S. coins and yet cannot be located in this book, which is complete insofar as U.S. coinage is concerned. Such pieces will no doubt turn out to be privately struck tokens of the 19th century. Enormous amounts of these were made during the late 1830's and early 1860's. In both cases the tokens were issued to relieve shortages of small change and they actually circulated as 1 Cent pieces; the early pieces being the size of large Cents and called "Hard Times Tokens"; the later pieces being the size of small Cents and called "Civil War Cents." Such tokens generally have a cash premium value of from $1.00 to $2.00 each.

Other coins which appear to be U.S. pieces are the so-called California gold coins. Like the tokens described above, they are not really coins but private issues; in neither case were they struck under authority of the U.S. Government, nor did they emanate from any government mint.

These California gold pieces—also called charms—exist in denominations of ¼, ½ and 1 Dollar; they may be round or they may be octagonal in shape; they are quite tiny and very thin and they may, or may not, be of gold; some of them have been restruck in recent years.

They were first made in the middle of the 19th Century, ostensibly to augment the gold coins then in circulation out west. It is doubtful if they ever served that purpose, because their minute size and insubstantial weight must have made them impossible to handle with any assurance of safety.

Those pieces are considered to be the original issues which are struck in genuine gold and have the word, "Dollar" or "Dol" as part of the denomination. In this case they have a value ranging from about $25.00 to $50.00. Any other pieces are worth considerably less.

APPRAISING AND SELLING YOUR COINS

If you have any U.S. coins or currency for sale or any Canadian coins, it would be prudent to acquaint yourself with the contents of this book, so that you can be better informed and be guided accordingly.

This book has been so prepared that by proper reference to the catalogue section as well as to this Preface and to the General Information which follows, you will be able to appraise your coins yourself and estimate their cash value with a fair degree of accuracy. The following points should be borne in mind when appraising and selling your coins:—

PRICE. **The cash premium values in this book reflect the approximate prices that established, professional coin dealers will pay for material. These values, which are averages, have been arrived at by a careful study of many years duration of market conditions and buying trends from coast to coast. Since the valuations are averages, the price actually offered may vary from the published values.**

SUPPLY. Sometimes a dealer will not wish to buy certain coins—

even high-premium pieces—because he has an ample supply of them at the time of offer. In this respect he is like any other merchant who has to exercise a certain amount of inventory control to keep him from getting unhealthily overstocked in any one item.

DEMAND. On the other hand, if your coins are popular issues and continually in demand, the dealer will be tempted to buy them even though he has an ample stock. In this case, he is taking a calculated risk, based on his experiences and judgment, and he is gambling either that the demand will continue strong or that the coins will enhance in value.

RARITY. In general, the higher the premium value of the coin, the easier it will be to sell. A coin with a value very much above its face value, or very much above the average for that type, will tend to be a scarce coin in short supply and hence in demand.

CONDITION. The values in this book are based on the condition in which the coins are most frequently found, namely, good to very good, as has been proven by experience. If your coins are in much choicer condition they will command a higher price than listed; if in inferior condition either a lower price, or no premium at all, will prevail. In some cases, as will be noted in the catalogue, the valuations are for uncirculated or proof specimens. In the case of all gold coins the valuations are for specimens in choice, well preserved condition, ranging from extremely fine to uncirculated.

CLEANING. As noted earlier, coins should be left in the same condition as when found. No attempt should be made to alter their appearance by cleaning or polishing.

COIN DEALERS. Coins and currency should be offered to professional coin dealers established in a regular place of business. For a list of the coin dealers in any community, consult the local classified telephone directory under the heading "Coin Dealers," or those Sunday newspapers that have a Stamp and Coin section and carry the advertising of coin dealers. The material you have may be brought to them in person or it may be shipped in for their inspection and offer, or a list of it may be sent by mail to see if they are interested.

MINT AND MINT MARKS—ABBREVIATIONS

The capital letters you will see after certain dates represent mint marks. They appear in this manner: 1853-O, 1878-S, 1890-CC, etc. The actual spot on the coin where the mint mark may be found is indicated clearly in the catalogue, before the listing of each type coin. The letters and the mints they represent are as follows (please remember that coins struck at the Philadelphia mint do not have a mint mark except as noted below):—

C—Charlotte, N.C. On gold coins only from 1838-1861.
CC—Carson City, Nev. On gold and silver coins from 1870-1893.
D—Dahlonega, Ga. On gold coins only from 1838-1861.
D—Denver, Colo. On all coins from 1906-1964, 1968 to date.
O—New Orleans, La. On gold and silver coins from 1838-1909.
P—Philadelphia, Pa. On nickels from 1942-1945. On Anthony dollars from 1979 to date. On nickels, dimes, quarters and half dollars from 1980 to date.
S—San Francisco, Calif. On all coins from 1854-1955, 1968 to date.

CANADIAN ISSUES

H—Heaton Mint in Birmingham, England.
C—Ottawa Mint in Canada.
No mint mark—Before 1908, London and after 1908, Ottawa.

Abbreviations for the condition of coins are given under the heading "Condition" (see above). Other abbreviations used are:
OBV.—Obverse or the "head" side of a coin.
REV.—Reverse or the "tail" side of a coin.
ARR.—Arrows, as on certain silver coins from 1853-1855 and 1873-1874.
In the General Information, which follows, you will find important data on various coins.

GENERAL INFORMATION

(Notes and comments on various coins, giving more specific or detailed information than is to be found in the catalogue proper.)

COLONIAL AND STATE COINAGE

Many of these coins are so rare, that forgeries have been created. There are various types of these forgeries, such as electrotypes, casts and struck copies. The last type is especially difficult to recognize since the forged piece is struck from an actual die manufactured for that purpose. In general, any very rare Colonial coin in really first class condition should be suspected of being a forgery or other type of facsimile, and all such pieces should be authenticated.

CAROLINA ELEPHANT TOKEN COINAGE. A very rare variety has the spelling "Proprieters." Forgeries exist.

CONNECTICUT. Higley Token Coinage. Forgeries exist. There is also a unique variety in which a wheel appears on the Rev. In the State Coinage, there are very many minor varieties in the appearance of the bust and in the spelling of the legends.

MARYLAND. Forgeries exist of the Lord Baltimore Penny, which is a very rare coin. The head on the 3 Pence piece of Standish Barry is reputed to be that of Washington. This coin has the date as "July 4, 90."

MASSACHUSETTS. Forgeries exist of the NE coinage and of the Oak Tree and Pine Tree issues. In the State Coinage there is a rare variety of the 1787 Cent in which the eagle holds the bundle of arrows in the right talon, rather than in the left one.

NEW ENGLAND COINAGE. The Elephant Half Penny of 1694 is similar in design to the Carolina Half Penny of 1694. The New England piece, however, is extremely rare and forgeries exist.

NEW HAMPSHIRE. Forgeries are known of the 1776 Cent.

NEW JERSEY. The St. Patrick coins, sometimes attributed to New Jersey, will be found in Part Two, since they bear nothing on them to identify them with New Jersey. A scarce variety of the 1788 Cent shows the horse's head facing to the left.

NEW YORK. Forgeries exist of the Cents of Gov. Clinton, of the "Non VI . . ." type, of the Indian type and of the Excelsior type. A unique specimen is known of a New York Cent which shows the head of George III on one side and a standing Indian on the other. There are several varieties of the 1787 Cent with laureate male bust. These varieties are called "Nova Eboracs" (New Yorks). The bust may differ in size or the seated figure may face either to right or left.

UNITED STATES OF AMERICA. The 1792 coinage of the U.S. Mint has traditionally been catalogued with Colonial Coins, the whole forming the subject of Early American Coins. The 1792 coins were experimental and all are very rare and seldom met with, except for the Half Disme. Regular U.S. coinage began in 1793. (The illustration of the 1792 Cent with silver center does not show the silver center.)

On the other hand, the Fugio Cents of 1787 were the first coins issued under the authority of the United States Government and were reportedly struck at New Haven. These actually circulated and are far commoner than the 1792 issues.

CONFEDERATIO COINAGE. Forgeries exist of the 1785 Cent.

THE CONTINENTAL DOLLAR. On some varieties, the word is spelled as "Curency." Forgeries and imitations are known.

NOVA CONSTELLATIO—IMMUNE COLUMBIA COINAGE. The "U.S." that appears on the Rev. of the 1783-1786 Cents may be either in block letters or in a script monogram. On some varieties the word is spelled as "Constelatio." Forgeries are known of the 1785 Cents inscribed "Immune Columbia."

THE TRIANGLE TOKEN. This piece has sometimes been called a Kentucky Cent, only because "K" appears at the top of the triangle of 15 rosettes, each bearing an initial of one of the 15 states. Otherwise, this coin does not bear the name of a specific colony.

GEORGE WASHINGTON COINS AND TOKENS. Forgeries are known of most valuable pieces including the 1792 Half Dollars.

UNITED STATES COINS

HALF CENTS. Various type forgeries are known of 1793 and 1796 and electrotype forgeries mainly of 1831, 1836, 1852, and 1840-1848 inclusive.

1797. A rare variety has lettering on the edge.

1808. A scarce variety shows the last 8 struck over a 7.

LARGE CENTS. 1793. All three major varieties of this date have been forged, mainly by electrotyping. "America" on the Chain type sometimes appears as "Ameri"; the wreath type has either lettering on the edge or vines and bars, and there is an extremely rare variety with a strawberry sprig under the head rather than a 3-leaf sprig.

1797. A scarce variety has a stemless wreath on the Rev.

1798. A scarce variety has the Rev. typical of 1796 Cents.

1799. This coin has been extensively forged by altering the date of another Large Cent of similar type to read 1799.

1801. A scarce variety has three errors in the design; there is but one stem to the wreath; the fraction appears as 1/000 and "United" as "Ilnited."

1804. This coin too has been forged by altering the date of another coin.

1815. Cents have been struck in every year from 1793 to date except 1815. In order to maintain an unbroken continuity of years, some collectors have altered other cents to read "1815." An 1815 Cent is therefore a fantasy created by self-delusion.

1839. A rare variety shows the 9 struck over a 6.

FLYING EAGLE CENTS. 1856. More forgeries must exist of this date than of any other U.S. coin. Most of these forgeries are altered dates, which are clearly visible under a strong magnifier; 1858 Cents have been used most often for this alteration, the last 8 being converted into a 6.

INDIAN HEAD CENTS. 1864-L. The L appears as a quite small letter at the end of the ribbon as it trails off the feather head dress on the Indian head.

LINCOLN HEAD CENTS. 1909-VDB. The VDB appears as three small letters at the extreme bottom of the Rev. They indicate the initials of the designer, Mr. Victor D. Brenner.

1914-D. This coin has recently been forged by alteration. A "D" has been added to a plain 1914 Cent or a D mint marked coin ending in a 4 has been changed to 1914.

2 CENT PIECES. 1864 Small Motto. This refers to "In God We Trust." The quickest way to distinguish the small letters in the motto from the large ones in the Large Motto type is to look at the letter D in God. In the Small Motto the D is quite rounded; in the large motto it is narrow and oval.

BUFFALO NICKELS. A scarce variety of 1918-D shows the 8 struck over a 7. The 3-legged buffalo of 1937-D shows the buffalo standing on only three legs, the result of a die defect obliterating the fourth leg.

HALF DIMES. 1796. A rare variety shows the 6 struck over the 5 of 1795.

1872-S. The mint mark may be either within or below the wreath.

DIMES. 1811. All coins are struck over 1809.

1823. All coins are struck over 1822.

1824. All coins are struck over 1822.

1873-CC. Only one specimen is known without arrows at the date.

1875. The S and CC mint marks may be either within or below the wreath.

1942/1. A scarce variety exists on which the 2 is struck over the 1 of 1941.

QUARTERS. 1822. A rare variety shows the 25c on the Rev. struck over 50c.

1823. All coins are struck over 1822.

1825. All coins are struck over other dates.

1828. A rare variety shows the 25c struck over 50c.

1842. A rare variety has a small date and exists in proof condition only.

1853/2. All coins are struck over 1852, and are without arrows. This coin has been forged by changing the last 8 of an 1858 into a 3.

1918-S/17. A scarce variety shows the 8 struck over the 7 of a 1917-S.

HALF DOLLARS. 1795. A rare variety shows a stem with three leaves, rather than two, on the upper part of the branch under each wing of the eagle.

1805-1836. Coins of these years are rich in varieties. There are overdates, small and large dates, small and large letters, etc.

1842-O. A rare variety exists with the date much smaller in size.

1846. A rare variety shows the 6 struck over another 6 at right angles to it.

1846-O. A scarce variety shows the date in much taller numerals.

1847. A rare variety shows the 7 struck over the 6 of an 1846.

1853-O without arrows or rays. This great rarity has been forged by altering the last 8 of an 1858-O to a 3.

1917. The mint marks may appear on the Obv. under the motto or on the Rev. to the left of "Half Dollar."

SILVER DOLLARS. 1797. A rare variety has the Rev. legend in smaller letters with a 9 x 7 arrangement of the stars on the Obv.

1895. This rare coin, which exists in proof condition only, has been forged by removing the mint marks on an 1895-O or 1895-S.

UNITED STATES PROOF SETS

The prices of proof sets are subject to some very sudden changes, either upward or downward. This is caused by the private accumulation of large amounts of sets and the resultant speculation therein.

U.S. SILVER COMMEMORATIVE COINS

GRANT 1922*. This coin has been forged by adding a star to an ordinary Grant Half Dollar. All Grant coins with star should be authenticated.

BOONE, 1934-1938. The small 1934 appears on all issues beginning with 1935. It will be found to the right of the standing figure on the Rev.

U.S. GOLD COMMEMORATIVE COINS

LEWIS AND CLARK ISSUE. The Gold Dollars of this issue tended to be used as jewelry. All specimens should be examined for evidence of loop removed or solder remains.

UNITED STATES GOLD COINS

1 DOLLAR. A minor variety appears in the 1849 coinage. The wreath on the Rev. may form a full circle or an open circle.

2½ DOLLARS. 1802. All coins are struck over 1801.

1806. All coins are struck over 1804 or 1805.

1824. All coins are struck over 1821.

1826. All coins are struck over 1825.

1841. This coin has been forged by removing the mint marks from 1841-C or 1841-D coins.

1854-S. This coin has been forged by adding an S mint mark to an 1854 coin of the Philadelphia Mint.

1863. This coin exists in proof condition only, but forgeries have been made by removing the S from 1863-S coins.

3 DOLLARS. 1873 and 1878. These dates should always be looked at under a magnifier. Many persons have accidentally misread these dates because the 3 and the 8 tend to look similar at first glance.

4 DOLLARS. These pieces should always be authenticated as being of gold. Genuine specimens struck from these dies in minor metals as patterns, have sometimes been gold plated as a deception or as an act of self-delusion.

5 DOLLARS. 1795, 1797 and 1798. These three dates each exist in two distinct types; please see the catalogue for proper attribution.

1802. All coins are struck over 1801.

1803. All coins are struck over 1802.

1825. All coins are struck over 1821 or 1824.

1807 and 1834. These two dates each exist in two distinct types.

1854-S. This very rare coin should always be verified as not being an 1854 Philadelphia coin to which an S has later been added.

1887. This coin was struck only in proof condition but forgeries have been made by removing the S mint mark from an 1887-S.

1909-O. This coin should be carefully examined to verify that the mint mark is genuine, or if genuine, that the O is not being mis-read for a D, since these mint marks are usually quite weak.

10 DOLLARS. 1797. This date exists in two distinct types.

1858. Forgeries have been created by removing the mint marks from 1858-O or 1858-S coins.

1907, 1908. These dates exist in more than one distinct type.

20 DOLLARS. 1861 and 1861-S. Each of these two coins exists as a great rarity when the Rev. design is the Paquet type. This type can be identified by the much taller letters in the legend.

1907, 1908. These dates exist in more than one distinct type.

All rare coins of the Philadelphia Mint should be examined for evidence of removed mint marks.

Rare date issues of the period 1908-1932 are subject to sudden price changes, as large amounts tend to be found unexpectedly from time to time.

In recent years, counterfeit coins, struck in gold, have appeared in all denominations, rare as well as common dates.

PIONEER GOLD COINS

The valuations are for coins in average VG-F condition. Really choice pieces are very rare and would command higher prices. If several varieties exist of a given coin, the valuation is for the commonest one.

NORRIS, GRIEG & NORRIS. A 5 Dollar piece has recently been discovered issued at Stockton rather than San Francisco.

TEMPLETON REID. The only known specimen of the 25 Dollar piece of 1849 was stolen in 1858 from the U.S. Mint collection and has never been recovered.

UNITED STATES PAPER MONEY
CONFEDERATE PAPER MONEY

The valuations given for the large size notes and Fractional Currency are for specimens in presentable, used condition (fine to very fine) and not giving a dirty, shopworn appearance. Notes which are torn, thin from use, very badly wrinkled or generally unattractive, would command a smaller premium than listed or none at all, since currency is collected mainly for the beauty and eye appeal inherent in well preserved specimens. Notes which are in new or unused condition would naturally be purchased at higher prices than listed.

Small size or present day notes, on the other hand, are valued in new condition only. Since the notes are recent and more readily available, they are not generally wanted in used condition.

Those who are interested in a fully illustrated book on U.S. paper money are referred to the standard work on this subject, "Paper Money of the United States" by Robert Friedberg. This complete and definitive volume illustrates front and back of every type of paper money ever issued from the 3 Cent note to the 10,000 Dollar note and from the first year of issue in 1861 to the present day. In addition, all varieties of seals and signatures are listed with collectors' valuations. "Paper Money of the United States" is available at almost any coin dealer or you may write for information to the publishers of this book.

There are many varieties of currency, formed by differences in the seals, signatures, series letters, etc., and in all cases, the valuations are for the commoner varieties.

THE COINAGE OF BRITISH NORTH AMERICA

This series begins with the Canadian issues of 1858, which were the first true coins based on the Canadian Dollar consisting of 100 Cents. Prior to 1858, the coinage in use consisted of a miscellaneous variety of copper tokens based on the English Pound. There are hundreds of varieties of these Penny and Half Penny tokens, most of them of only small value (from about .10 to .50) and they are omitted from this book because they are not considered as coins.

Following the introduction of Canadian coins in 1858, the first coins of Newfoundland were issued in 1865, and of Nova Scotia and New Brunswick in 1861. The only issue of Prince Edward Island was a 1 Cent piece in 1871 and of British Columbia a 10 and 20 Dollar gold piece in 1862. These gold coins, however, were not placed in circulation because of opposition from England.

As with the U.S. coins, the valuations for Canadian coins are based on G-VG condition except where otherwise stated.

In 1936 a small dot was placed under the date on some of the 1, 10 and 25 Cent pieces struck in that year. 25 Cent pieces with the dot are somewhat scarce, but the 1 and 10 Cent pieces are very rare.

The maple leaf on part of the 1947 coinage of all denominations may be found as a quite small symbol to the immediate right of the date.

CANADIAN COIN VARIETIES. There are some variations from the normal among certain Canadian coins, making them of greater scarcity and value. The most important varieties follow.

1 Cent 1859. Struck over 1858.

1 Cent 1891. With a smaller date than normal.

1 Cent 1936. With dot below date.

5 Cents 1858. With a larger date than normal.

5 Cents 1900. With round O's in date rather than oval.

5 Cents 1902-H. With a smaller H mint mark than normal.

5 Cents 1921. Not a variety but very rare as a coin because most of the 2½ million struck were melted down rather than issued.

10 Cents 1893. With the top part of the 3 rounded rather than flat.

10 Cents 1913. With larger leaves on the Rev. than normal.

10 Cents 1936. With dot below date.

25 Cents 1936. With dot below the wreath under date.

50 Cents 1921. Like the 5 Cents 1921, not a variety but very rare as a coin because most were melted down.

50 Cents 1946. With part of the design extending into the 6.

50 Cents 1947. With maple leaf and a curved 7 pointing to the right, rather than a straight 7 pointing to the left.

1 Dollar 1947. With a pointed 7 rather than a blunt 7 in the date.

Colonial and State Coinage

PART ONE

Coins and tokens issued by or for specific colonies or states. These pieces bear either a state name or a device that identifies the state. The valuations below are for coins in used or circulated condition. Bent and holed coins are worthless.

Collectors should be aware that many of the following pieces exist as casts and electrotypes. These are also worthless.

CAROLINA ELEPHANT TOKEN COINAGE

Elephant. Rev. "GOD PRESERVE CAROLINA AND THE LORDS PROPRIETORS 1694." Copper.

Half Penny 1694... **600.00**

CONNECTICUT

Higley Token Coinage

Deer standing. Rev. Three axes. Copper.

3 Pence 1737 .... **2,500.00**

Deer standing. Rev. One large axe. Copper.

3 Pence. No date, 1739.. **4,000.00**

State Coinage

Laureate bust facing right or left. Rev. Female seated. Copper.

1 Cent 1785, 1786, 1787, 1788 .... **15.00**

KENTUCKY
Myddelton Token Coinage

Liberty stretching hand out to two children. Rev. Female seated with shield.

1 Cent 1796. Struck in copper **600.00**
1 Cent 1796. Struck in silver **500.00**

MARYLAND

Cecil Calvert (Lord Baltimore) Coinage

Head of Lord Baltimore. Rev. Crowned shield and Roman numeral. Silver.

1 Shilling. No date (1658)... **400.00**
6 Pence. No date (1658)... **200.00**
4 Pence. No date (1658)... **500.00**

Head of Lord Baltimore. Rev. Two flags over crown. Copper.

1 Penny (Denarium). No date (1658) .... **Very Rare**

Annapolis Token Coinage of John Chalmers

Clasped hands in wreath. Two birds and snake within circle. Silver.

1 Shilling 1783 .... **200.00**

Clasped hands. Rev. Circle of rings. Silver.

1 Shilling 1783 .... **Very Rare**

Long cross. Rev. Wreath. Silver.

6 Pence 1783 .... **400.00**

Clasped hands. Rev. Plant in wreath. Silver.

3 Pence 1783 .... **375.00**

Baltimore Token Coinage of Standish Barry

Large male head. Rev. Name and value. Silver.

3 Pence 1790 .... **Very Rare**

MASSACHUSETTS
NE (New England) Coinage

NE at top, the rest blank. Rev. Roman numeral for value at top,
the rest blank. Silver.

1 Shilling. No date (1652).. **2,000.00**
6 Pence. No date (1652).. ——
3 Pence. No date (1652).. ——

Willow Tree Coinage

A willow tree. Rev. Date and Roman numeral for the value. Silver.

1 Shilling 1652	**3,500.00**
6 Pence 1652	⸻
3 Pence 1652	⸻

Oak Tree Coinage

An oak tree. Rev. Date and Roman numeral for the value. Silver.

1 Shilling 1652	**100.00**
6 Pence 1652	**100.00**
3 Pence 1652	**100.00**
2 Pence 1662	**100.00**

Pine Tree Coinage

A pine tree. Rev. Date and Roman numeral for the value. Silver.

1 Shilling 1652. Large size	**100.00**
1 Shilling 1652. Small size	**100.00**
6 Pence 1652	**75.00**
3 Pence 1652	**70.00**

State Coinage

Pine tree. Rev. Female seated on globe. Copper.

1 Cent 1776 .... **Unique**

Three heads in Janiform position. Rev. Female seated on globe. Copper.

Half Penny 1776 .... **Unique**

Indian standing. Rev. Spread eagle. Copper.

1 Cent 1787, 1788 ....   15.00
Half Cent 1787, 1788 ....   17.50

NEW ENGLAND COINAGE
Elephant Token Coinage

Elephant. Rev. "GOD PRESERVE NEW ENGLAND 1694." Copper.

Half Penny 1694 .... **Very Rare**

Lion Token Coinage

Two lions facing in opposite directions. Rev. "NEW ENGLAND." Copper.
Token coin. No date (1675)... **500.00**

NEW HAMPSHIRE

Pine tree. Rev. Harp. Copper.
1 Cent 1776.. **3,000.00**

NEW JERSEY

Horse's head and plow with date below plow. Rev. Shield. Copper.
1 Cent 1786, 1787, 1788 .... **15.00**

Horse's head and plow with date to right of plow. Rev. Shield. Copper.
1 Cent 1786.. **25.00**

Head of Washington. Rev. Spread eagle. Copper.
1 Cent. No date (1786) .... ——

Head of Washington. Rev. Shield. Copper.
1 Cent. No date (1786) .... ——

Liberty holding scales, "Immunis Columbia." Rev. Shield. Copper.
1 Cent 1786.. ——

Spread eagle. Rev. Shield. Copper.
1 Cent 1786.. ——

NEW YORK

State Copper Coinage

Bust of Gov. Clinton. Rev. Shield supported by two figures.
1 Cent 1787.. **2,000.00**

Laureate male bust. Rev. Female seated to right or left.

1 Cent 1787.. **30.00**

Armored bust, "NON VI VIRTUTE VICI." Rev. Liberty holding scales.

1 Cent 1786.. **1,500.00**

Liberty holding scales, "IMMUNIS COLUMBIA." Rev. Eagle.

1 Cent 1787.. **100.00**

Indian standing. Rev. Eagle on globe.

1 Cent 1787.. **1,500.00**

Indian standing. Rev. Shield supported by two figures.

1 Cent 1787 .... **1,500.00**

Shield supported by two figures. Rev. Eagle. The EXCELSIOR cent.

1 Cent 1787 .... **300.00**

Miscellaneous Token Coinage
New Yorke in America Token

Spread eagle. Rev. Two figures under palm tree.

Brass token. No date (1700) **1,000.00**

The Mott Token

Large clock. Rev. Eagle. Copper.

Token 1 Cent 1789 .... **40.00**

Talbot, Allum & Lee Token

Liberty standing. Rev. Ship. Copper.

1 Cent 1794, 1795 .... **15.00**

RHODE ISLAND

Admiral Howe's flagship. Rev. Group of ships.

Copper Token 1778, 1779 ....,............... **100.00**

UNITED STATES OF AMERICA

FUGIO CENT COINAGE

Sundial, radiate sun above, and "MIND YOUR BUSINESS" below.
Rev. Circular chain of thirteen links.

1 Cent 1787 .... **20.00**

EARLY MINT ISSUES

Liberty head. Rev. Flying eagle.

1 Disme 1792. Silver.. ——
1 Disme 1792. Copper.. ——
Half Disme 1792. Silver **600.00**

Liberty head. Rev. Wreath. With silver center plug.

1 Cent 1792.. **500.00**

*Liberty head. Rev. Wreath. The so called Birch Cent, and much
larger than the above cent.*

1 Cent 1792.. **Very Rare**

U.S.A. BAR CENT

Monogram of USA. Rev. Thirteen bars. Copper.
1 Cent. No date (1785) **150.00**

VERMONT

Hills over plow. Rev. Radiate eye. Copper.
1 Cent 1785, 1786.. **45.00**

Male bust. Rev. Seated female, "IMMUNE COLUMBIA." Copper.
1 Cent 1785.. **1,000.00**

Male bust to right or left. Rev. Seated female. Copper.
1 Cent 1786, 1787, 1788 .... **45.00**

VIRGINIA

Gloucester Token Coinage

Building. Rev. Star. Brass.
1 Shilling 1714 .... **Very Rare**

English Royal Coinage

Head of George III. Rev. Arms and date.

1 Shilling 1774. Silver .... **Very Rare**
1 Penny 1773. Copper .... **Rare**
Half Penny 1773. Copper **15.00**

PART II

Coins and tokens issued for general use in early America and not inscribed with the name of any specific colony or state.

AUCTORI PLEBIS TOKEN COINAGE

Male bust, "AUCTORI PLEBIS." Rev. Seated female. Copper.

1 Cent 1787 .... **25.00**

CONFEDERATIO COINAGE

*Figure at pedestal holding bow and arrow. Rev. Thirteen stars in
radiate circle. Copper.*

1 Cent 1785 .... **Rare**

THE CONTINENTAL DOLLAR

*Sundial with radiate sun above. Rev. The names of the thirteen states
inscribed on the links of a circular chain. Many copies exist.*

1 Dollar 1776. Struck in pewter	**600.00**
1 Dollar 1776. Struck in brass	——
1 Dollar 1776. Struck in silver	——

GEORGE III—IMMUNE COLUMBIA COINAGE

Head of George III. Rev. Liberty holding scales, "IMMUNE COLUMBIA." Copper.

1 Cent 1785..	**700.00**

GEORGIUS TRIUMPHO TOKEN COINAGE

Laureate male head. Rev. Liberty standing behind screen of thirteen bars. Copper.

1 Cent token 1783...	**35.00**

NORTH AMERICAN TOKEN

Seated female (Hibernia). Rev. Ship. Copper.

Token coin 1781 .... **17.50**

NOVA CONSTELLATIO—IMMUNE COLUMBIA COINAGE

Radiate eye. Rev. "U.S." in wreath. Copper.
(The U.S. in either block or script letters)

1 Cent 1783, 1785, 1786 .... **20.00**

Radiate eye. Rev. Liberty holding scales, "IMMUNE COLUMBIA."

1 Cent 1785. Copper.. **Rare**
1 Cent 1785. Struck in silver .... ——

PITT TOKEN COINAGE

Bust of William Pitt. Rev. Ship and "AMERICA." Copper.

Half Penny 1766... **125.00**
1 Farthing 1766... ——

PLANTATION TOKEN COINAGE

*Horseman and titles of James II of England. Rev. Four shields. Pewter. (This
token is sometimes attributed to Florida, but was used in many colonies.)*

1/24th Part Real 1688 .... **50.00**

ST. PATRICK COINAGE OF MARK NEWBY

(Used Mainly in New Jersey)

St. Patrick standing before throng. Rev. Crowned figure playing harp.

Half Penny. No date (1678). Copper.. **65.00**

*St. Patrick holding cross, snakes in foreground. Rev. Crowned
figure playing harp.*

1 Farthing. No date (1678). Copper.. **35.00**
1 Farthing. Same but struck in silver **300.00**

THE TRIANGLE TOKEN

*Hand holding scroll. Rev. Triangle formed by fifteen stars, each bearing
the initial of a state. K for Kentucky is at top. Copper.*

1 Cent. No date (1792) **25.00**

VOCE POPULI—HIBERNIA COINAGE

Male bust. Rev. Seated female and "HIBERNIA." Copper.

Half Penny 1760.. **5.00**
1 Farthing 1760.. **20.00**

WOOD'S COINAGE—HIBERNIA TYPE

Head of George I. Rev. Seated female with harp. Copper.

Half Penny 1722, 1723, 1724 .... **15.00**
1 Fathing 1722, 1723, 1724.. **25.00**

WOOD'S COINAGE—ROSA AMERICANA TYPE

Head of George I. Rev. Rose. Copper.

2 Pence 1722, 1723 or no date	**45.00**
1 Penny 1722, 1723..	**35.00**
Half Penny 1722, 1723..	**35.00**

PART III

GEORGE WASHINGTON COINS AND TOKENS

(All are copper except the Half Dollars of 1792)

Obv: Military bust. "WASHINGTON & INDEPENDENCE."
Rev: Liberty seated. "UNITED STATES."

1 Cent 1783...   **15.00**

Obv: Head. "WASHINGTON & INDEPENDENCE."
Rev: Liberty seated. "UNITED STATES."

1 Cent 1783...   **15.00**

Obv: Head. "WASHINGTON & INDEPENDENCE."
Rev: Wreath. "UNITY STATES OF AMERICA."

1 Cent 1783...   **20.00**

Obv: Military bust. "WASHINGTON."
Rev: Same bust. "ONE CENT."

1 Cent. No date (1783) **25.00**

Obv: Bust. "WASHINGTON PRESIDENT."
Rev: Large or small eagle. "ONE CENT."

1 Cent 1791... **65.00**

Obv: Bust. "WASHINGTON PRESIDENT."
Rev: Ship. "LIVERPOOL HALFPENNY."

Half Penny 1791... **300.00**

Obv: Bust. "WASHINGTON PRESIDENT."
Rev: Large spread eagle. No legend.

1 Cent 1792.. **Rare**

Obv: Laureate Roman-type head to right. "WASHINGTON PRESIDENT."
Rev: Eagle. "CENT."

1 Cent 1792.. **Rare**

Obv: Bust. "WASHINGTON PRESIDENT."
Rev: In ten lines, "GENERAL OF THE AMERICAN ARMIES 1775.
RESIGNED 1788. PRESIDENT OF THE UNITED STATES 1789."

1 Cent 1792.. **Rare**

Obv: Bust. "GEO. WASHINGTON BORN VIRGINIA FEBRUARY 11, 1732."
Rev: In ten lines, "GENERAL OF THE AMERICAN ARMIES 1775.
RESIGNED 1788. PRESIDENT OF THE UNITED STATES 1789."

1 Cent. No date (1792) .... **Rare**

Obv: Bust. "G. WASHINGTON PRESIDENT."
Rev: Small eagle, stars above. "UNITED STATES OF AMERICA."

Half Dollar 1792. Struck in silver .... —

Half Dollar 1792. Struck in copper.. —

Half Dollar 1792. Struck in silver. Similar to above but Rev. has

larger eagle and is without stars... —

Obv: Bust. "WASHINGTON PRESIDENT."
Rev: Ship. "HALFPENNY."

Half Penny 1793... **25.00**

Obv: Bust right. "GEORGE WASHINGTON."
Rev: Eagle over shield. "LIBERTY AND SECURITY 1795."

1 Penny 1795... **200.00**

Half penny 1795 .... **50.00**

Obv: Bust left. "GEORGE WASHINGTON."
Rev: Eagle over shield. "LIBERTY AND SECURITY."

1 Penny. No date (1795) **75.00**

Obv: Bust. "G. WASHINGTON FIRST FRIEND TO PEACE. . . ."
Rev: Grate, legend around edge and "LONDON 1795."
1 Cent 1795. The Grate Cent **40.00**

Obv: Bust. "GEORGE WASHINGTON."
Rev: Circle of fifteen stars. "SUCCESS TO THE UNITED STATES."
Success Token. No date (1795). Large size **50.00**
Success Token. As above but small size **50.00**

Obv: Bust. "GEORGIUS WASHINGTON."
Rev: Crowned harp. "NORTH WALES."
Half Penny. No date (1795) **50.00**

The valuations listed in this book closely approximate how much established coin dealers will pay for any material needed in their stock.

United States Coins

HALF CENTS

Type: Liberty head with cap facing left.

Date	Amount Minted	Value	Date	Amount Minted	Value
1793	31,900	650.00			

Type: Liberty head with cap facing right.

Date	Amount Minted	Value	Date	Amount Minted	Value
1794	81,600	100.00	1796	115,500	1,000.00
1795	25,600	75.00	1797	107,000	75.00

Type: Draped bust of Liberty.

Date	Amount Minted	Value	Date	Amount Minted	Value
1800	211,500	15.00	1805	814,500	15.00
1802	14,400	100.00	1806	356,000	15.00
1803	97,900	15.00	1807	476,000	15.00
1804	1 million	15.00	1808	400,000	15.00

Type: Liberty head in turban.

Date	Amount Minted	Value	Date		Amount Minted	Value
1809	1¼ million	13.50	1831	Proof Only	2,200	1,400.00
1810	0215,000	17.00	1832		154,000	13.50
1811	63,100	40.00	1833		120,000	13.50
1825	63,000	13.50	1834		141,000	13.50
1826	234,000	13.50	1835		398,000	13.50
1828	606,000	13.50	1836	Proof Only	——	1,200.00
1829	487,000	13.50				

Type: Liberty head with braided hair.

Date		Value	Date	Amount Minted	Value
1840		1,200.00	1849	39,900	15.00
1841		1,200.00	1850	39,800	14.00
1842		1,200.00	1851	147,700	14.00
1843	Only proofs were	1,200.00	1852	Proof only	1,300.00
1844	struck of these coins.	1,200.00	1853	129,700	14.00
1845	The exact quantities	1,200.00	1854	55,400	14.00
1846	minted are not known.	1,200.00	1855	56,500	14.00
1847		1,200.00	1856	40,400	14.00
1848		1,200.00	1857	35,200	17.00
1849		1,200.00			

(The valuations in this book are based on the coins being in G-VG condition, unless otherwise noted.)

LARGE CENTS

Type: Liberty head with close flowing hair; chain on Rev.

Date	Amount Minted	Value	Date	Amount Minted	Value
1793	——	**650.00**	(About 224,000 were coined of all types of 1793 cents)		

Type: Liberty head with loose flowing hair; wreath on Rev.

1793		400.00	(See above)

Type: Liberty head with cap.

1793	(See above)	310.00	1795	82,000	25.00
1794	918,500	30.00	1796	Part of 974,700	35.00

Large Cents (continued)

Type: Draped bust of Liberty.

Date	Amount Minted	Value	Date	Amount Minted	Value
1796	Part of 974,700	30.00	1802	3½ million	10.00
1797	897,500	16.00	1803	2½ million	11.00
1798	979,700	15.00	1804	756,800	150.00
1799	904,600	300.00	1805	941,100	11.00
1800	2¾ million	12.00	1806	348,000	15.00
1801	1⅓ million	12.00	1807	727,200	11.00

Type: Liberty head in turban.

Date	Amount Minted	Value	Date	Amount Minted	Value
1808	1 million	16.00	1812	1 million	15.00
1809	222,900	35.00	1813	418,000	19.00
1810	1½ million	15.00	1814	357,800	15.00
1811	218,000	20.00			

Type: Liberty head in coronet.

Date	Amount Minted	Value	Date	Amount Minted	Value
1816	2¾ million	4.50	1818	3¼ million	4.25
1817	4 million	4.25	1819	2⅔ million	4.25

Date	Amount Minted	Value	Date	Amount Minted	Value
1820	4½ million	4.25	1828	2¼ million	4.25
1821	389,000	8.00	1829	1½ million	4.25
1822	2 million	4.25	1830	1¾ million	4.25
1823	855,700	15.00	1831	3⅓ million	4.00
1824	1¼ million	4.25	1832	2⅓ million	4.00
1825	1½ million	4.25	1833	2¾ million	4.00
1826	1½ million	4.25	1834	2 million	4.25
1827	2⅓ million	4.25	1835	Part of 4 million	4.00

Type: Liberty head with braided hair.

Date	Amount Minted	Value	Date	Amount Minted	Value
1835	Part of 4 million	4.00	1847	6¼ million	4.00
1836	2 million	4.00	1848	6½ million	4.00
1837	5½ million	4.00	1849	4¼ million	4.00
1838	6⅓ million	4.00	1850	4½ million	4.00
1839	3¼ million	4.00	1851	10 million	4.00
1840	2½ million	4.00	1852	5 million	4.00
1841	1½ million	4.00	1853	6⅔ million	4.00
1842	2⅓ million	4.00	1854	4¼ million	4.00
1843	2½ million	4.00	1855	1½ million	4.00
1844	2½ million	4.00	1856	2⅔ million	4.00
1845	4 million	4.00	1857	333,500	12.00
1846	4 million	4.00			

SMALL CENTS

Type: Flying eagle—Copper-Nickel

Date	Amount Minted	Value	Date	Amount Minted	Value
1856	About 1000	600.00	1858	24⅔ million	5.00
1857	17½ million	5.00			

Type: Indian head; without shield on Rev.—Copper-Nickel

Date	Amount Minted	Value
1859	36⅓ million	**2.75**

Type: Indian head; with shield on Rev.—Copper-Nickel

Date	Amount Minted	Value	Date	Amount Minted	Value
1860	20½ million	**1.90**	1863	49¾ million	**1.75**
1861	10 million	**4.00**	1864	13¾ million	**2.75**
1862	28 million	**1.75**			

(The bronze Indian Head Cents which follow are of the same design as the Copper-Nickel Cents above)

Type: Indian head—Bronze

(The "S" mint mark of 1908 and 1909 is on the Rev., under the wreath)

Date	Amount Minted	Value	Date	Amount Minted	Value
1864	39¼ million	1.75	1884	23¼ million	.85
1864-L	Part of above	15.00	1885	11¾ million	1.50
1865	35½ million	1.75	1886	17⅔ million	.85
1866	9¾ million	12.00	1887	45¼ million	.40
1867	9¾ million	12.00	1888	37½ million	.40
1868	10¼ million	12.00	1889	48¾ million	.40
1869	6½ million	15.00	1890	57¼ million	.40
1870	5¼ million	12.00	1891	47 million	.40
1871	4 million	17.00	1892	37⅔ million	.40
1872	4 million	20.00	1893	46⅔ million	.40
1873	11⅔ million	4.00	1894	16¾ million	.75
1874	14¼ million	4.00	1895	38⅓ million	.35
1875	13½ million	4.00	1896	39 million	.35
1876	8 million	6.00	1897	50½ million	.35
1877	852,500	150.00	1898	49¾ million	.35
1878	5¾ million	6.00	1899	53⅔ million	.35
1879	16¼ million	1.25	1900	66¾ million	.30
1880	39 million	.75	1901	79⅔ million	.30
1881	39¼ million	.75	1902	87⅓ million	.30
1882	38½ million	.75	1903	85 million	.30
1883	45½ million	.75	1904	61⅓ million	.30

Date	Amount Minted	Value	Date	Amount Minted	Value
1905	80¾ million	.30	1908-S	1 million	12.00
1906	96 million	.30	1909	14⅓ million	.40
1907	108¼ million	.30	1909-S	309,000	60.00
1908	32⅓ million	.30			

Type: Lincoln head

(The mint mark is on the Obv., under the date)

Date	Amount Minted	Value	Date	Amount Minted	Value
1909-VDB	28 million	.75	1919	392 million	.03
1909-S-VDB	484,000	170.00	1919-D	57¼ million	.07
1909	72¾ million	.10	1919-S	139¾ million	.07
1909-S	1¾ million	30.00	1920	310¼ million	.03
1910	146¾ million	.05	1920-D	49⅓ million	.05
1910-S	6 million	4.00	1920-S	46¼ million	.05
1911	101¼ million	.05	1921	39¼ million	.05
1911-D	12¾ million	2.00	1921-S	15⅓ million	.30
1911-S	4 million	6.50	1922-D	7¼ million	2.50
1912	68¼ million	.05	1922 Plain Part of above		125.00
1912-D	10½ million	2.00	1923	74¾ million	.03
1912-S	4½ million	5.75	1923-S	8¾ million	.75
1913	76½ million	.05	1924	75¼ million	.03
1913-D	15¾ million	1.00	1924-D	2½ million	7.00
1913-S	6 million	4.00	1924-S	11¾ million	.25
1914	75¼ million	.05	1925	140 million	.03
1914-D	1¼ million	45.00	1925-D	22⅔ million	.05
1914-S	4 million	5.00	1925-S	26½ million	.05
1915	29 million	.20	1926	157 million	.03
1915-D	22 million	.15	1926-D	28 million	.05
1915-S	4¾ million	4.50	1926-S	4⅔ million	1.75
1916	131¾ million	.03	1927	144½ million	.03
1916-D	36 million	.07	1927-D	27¼ million	.05
1916-S	22½ million	.15	1927-S	14⅓ million	.15
1917	196½ million	.03	1928	134 million	.03
1917-D	55 million	.05	1928-D	31¼ million	.05
1917-S	32⅔ million	.05	1928-S	17⅓ million	.10
1918	288 million	.02	1929	185⅓ million	.03
1918-D	47¾ million	.07	1929-D	41¾ million	.03
1918-S	34¾ million	.07	1929-S	50 million	.03

Date	Amount Minted	Value	Date	Amount Minted	Value
1930	157½ million	.03	1944-S	282¾ million	.02
1930-D	40 million	.03	1945	1 billion	.02
1930-S	24⅓ million	.04	1945-D	226⅓ million	.02
1931	19½ million	.08	1945-S	181¾ million	.02
1931-D	4½ million	1.25	1946	991¾ million	.02
1931-S	866,000	22.00	1946-D	315¾ million	.02
1932	9 million	.60	1946-S	198 million	.02
1932-D	10½ million	.20	1947	190½ million	.02
1933	14½ million	.15	1947-D	194¾ million	.02
1933-D	6¼ million	.90	1947-S	99 million	.02
1934	219 million	.02	1948	317⅔ million	.02
1934-D	28½ million	.05	1948-D	172⅔ million	.02
1935	245½ million	.02	1948-S	81¾ million	.02
1935-D	47 million	.03	1949	217½ million	.02
1935-S	38¾ million	.03	1949-D	154⅓ million	.02
1936	309⅔ million	.02	1949-S	64⅓ million	.02
1936-D	40⅔ million	.03	1950	272¾ million	.02
1936-S	29 million	.04	1950-D	335 million	.02
1937	309¼ million	.02	1950-S	118½ million	.02
1937-D	50½ million	.03	1951	294⅔ million	.02
1937-S	34½ million	.04	1951-D	625½ million	.02
1938	156¾ million	.02	1951-S	101 million	.02
1938-D	20 million	.05	1952	187 million	.02
1938-S	15¼ million	.12	1952-D	746 million	.02
1939	316½ million	.02	1952-S	137¾ million	.02
1939-D	15¼ million	.12	1953	257 million	.02
1939-S	52 million	.03	1953-D	700½ million	.02
1940	586¾ million	.02	1953-S	182 million	.02
1940-D	81½ million	.02	1954	72 million	.02
1940-S	113 million	.02	1954-D	251½ million	.02
1941	887 million	.02	1954-S	96¼ million	.02
1941-D	128¾ million	.02	1955	331 million	.02
1941-S	92½ million	.02	1955 double die. (Very Fine)		190.00
1942	657¾ million	02	1955-D	563⅓ million	.02
1942-D	206¾ million	.02	1955-S	44⅔ million	.10
1942-S	85⅔ million	.02	1956	421 million	.02
1943	684⅔ million	.02	1956-D	1 billion	.02
1943-D	217¾ million	.02	1957	282½ million	.02
1943-S	191⅔ million	.03	1957-D	1 billion	.02
1944	1½ billion	.02	1958	252½ million	.02
1944-D	430⅔ million	.02	1958-D	801 million	.02

(The valuations in this book are based on the coins being in G-VG condition, unless otherwise noted.)

Type: Lincoln head with the Lincoln Memorial on the reverse.

Date	Amount Minted	Value	Date	Amount Minted	Value
1959	609¾ million	.01	1972-D	2⅔ billion	.01
1959-D	1¼ billion	.01	1972-S	380 million	.01
1960	586½ million	.01	1973	3¾ billion	.01
1960	Small Date (unc)	2.00	1973-D	3½ billion	.01
1960-D	1½ billion	.01	1973-S	320 million	.01
1960-D	Small Date	.01	1974	4¼ billion	.01
1961	753⅓ million	.01	1974-D	4¼ billion	.01
1961-D	1¾ billion	.01	1974-S	412 million	.01
1962	606 million	.01	1975	5½ billion	.01
1962-D	1¾ billion	.01	1975-D	4½ billion	.01
1963	754 million	.01	1975-S	proof only 3 million	5.00
1963-D	1¾ billion	.01	1976	4½ billion	.01
1964	2⅔ billion	.01	1976-D	4¼ billion	.01
1964-D	3¾ billion	.01	1976-S	proof only 4 million	1.50
1965	1½ billion	.01	1977	4½ billion	.01
1966	2¼ billion	.01	1977-D	4¼ billion	.01
1967	3 billion	.01	1977-S	proof only 3¼ million	1.50
1968	1¾ billion	.01	1978	5½ billion	.01
1968-D	2¾ billion	.01	1978-D	4¼ billion	.01
1968-S	258¼ million	.01	1978-S	proof only 3 million	2.00
1969	1⅕ billion	.01	1979	6 billion	.01
1969-D	4 billion	.01	1979-D	4¼ billion	.01
1969-S	544⅓ million	.01	1979-S	proof only 3¾ million	2.00
1970	1¾ billion	.01	1980	7½ billion	.01
1970-D	2¾ billion	.01	1980-D	5 billion	.01
1970-S	690½ million	.01	1980-S	proof only 3½ million	2.75
1970-S	Small Date (unc)	3.00	1981	7½ billion	.01
1971	2 billion	.01	1981-D	5½ billion	.01
1971-D	3 billion	.01	1981-S	proof only 4 million	2.50
1971-S	525 million	.01	1982		.01
1972	3 billion	.01	1982-D		.01
1972	double die. (unc)	150.00	1982-S	proof only	2.50

2 CENT PIECES

Type: Bronze with shield on Obv. and the value on the Rev.

Date	Amount Minted	Value	Date	Amount Minted	Value
1864 Large motto	19¾ million	3.00	1869	1½ million	3.25
1864 Small motto	Part of above	30.00	1870	861,250	3.75
1865	13⅔ million	3.00	1871	721,250	4.00
1866	3¼ million	3.00	1872	65,000	30.00
1867	3 million	3.00	1873	600 proofs	700.00
1868	3 million	3.00			

3 CENT PIECES—NICKEL

Type: Liberty head. The Rev. has the Roman numeral III for the value.

Date	Amount Minted	Value	Date	Amount Minted	Value
1865	11⅓ million	3.00	1878	2,350 proofs	800.00
1866	4¾ million	3.00	1879	41,200	20.00
1867	4 million	3.00	1880	25,000	25.00
1868	3¼ million	3.00	1881	1⅛ million	3.00
1869	1⅔ million	3.00	1882	25,300	25.00
1870	1⅓ million	3.00	1883	10,600	30.00
1871	604,000	3.25	1884	5,650	40.00
1872	862,000	3.25	1885	4,800	45.00
1873	1¼ million	3.00	1886	4,300 proofs	750.00
1874	790,000	3.25	1887	7,960	40.00
1875	228,000	3.75	1888	41,000	22.50
1876	162,000	3.75	1889	21,600	25.00
1877	510 proofs	1,000.00			

3 CENT PIECES—SILVER

Plain star and plain III
1851-1853

Star with borders; sprig and arrows of the III
1854-1873

Type: Large star, the Rev. has the Roman Numeral III for the value.

(The "O" mint mark is on the Rev., to the right of the III)

Date	Amount Minted	Value	Date	Amount Minted	Value
1851	5½ million	4.00	1862	363,550	5.00
1851-O	720,000	7.00	1863	21,500 proofs	300.00
1852	18⅔ million	4.00	1864	470 "	300.00
1853	11½ million	4.00	1865	8,500 "	300.00
1854	671,000	6.00	1866	22,700 "	300.00
1855	139,000	8.00	1867	4,625 "	300.00
1856	1½ million	4.50	1868	4,100 "	300.00
1857	1 million	4.50	1869	5,100 "	300.00
1858	1⅔ million	4.50	1870	4,000 "	300.00
1859	365,000	5.00	1871	4,260 "	300.00
1860	287,000	5.00	1872	1,950 "	300.00
1861	498,000	5.00	1873	600 "	600.00

NICKELS

Without rays on Rev.
1866-1867

Without rays on Rev.
1867-1883

Type: Shield. The U.S. shield is on the obv. and the value is on the Rev.

Date	Amount Minted	Value	Date	Amount Minted	Value
1866	14¾ million	4.25	1875	2 million	6.25
1867 With rays	3 million	4.50	1876	2½ million	4.50
1867 No rays	Part of above	4.00	1877	510 proofs	1,200.00
1868	28¾ million	4.00	1878	2,350 proofs	700.00
1869	16½ million	4.25	1879	29,100	50.00
1870	4¾ million	4.25	1880	19,950	55.00
1871	561,000	15.00	1881	72,400	45.00
1872	6 million	4.00	1882	11½ million	4.00
1873	4½ million	4.00	1883	1½ million	4.25
1874	3½ million	4.50			

Without "Cents" on Rev.
1883

With "Cents" on Rev.
1883-1913

Type: Liberty head.

(The mint marks of 1912 are on the Rev., to the left of "Cents" and under the dot)

Date	Amount Minted	Value	Date	Amount Minted	Value
1883 Without "Cents"	5½ million	1.00	1890	16¼ million	1.75
1883 With "Cents"	16 million	3.00	1891	16¾ million	1.50
1884	11¼ million	3.50	1892	11½ million	1.60
1885	1½ million	175.00	1893	13⅓ million	1.50
1886	3⅓ million	25.00	1894	5½ million	2.25
1887	15¼ million	2.25	1895	10 million	1.00
1888	10¾ million	3.25	1896	8¾ million	1.00
1889	15¾ million	1.50	1897	20½ million	.25

Date	Amount Minted	Value	Date	Amount Minted	Value
1898	12½ million	.25	1909	11½ million	.20
1899	26 million	.25	1910	30¼ million	.20
1900	27¼ million	.20	1911	39½ million	.20
1901	26½ million	.20	1912	26¼ million	.20
1902	31½ million	.20	1912-D	8½ million	.30
1903	28 million	.20	1912-S	238,000	20.00
1904	21½ million	.20	1913	5 pieces struck. All are	
1905	29¾ million	.20		accounted for in collec-	
1906	38⅔ million	.20		tions and it is not pos-	
1907	39¼ million	.20		sible to find one.	
1908	22⅔ million	.20			

Type I. Buffalo on hilly mound
1913

Type II. Buffalo on more level mound
1913-1938

Type: *Buffalo and Indian head.*

(The mint marks are on the Rev., under "Five Cents")

Date	Amount Minted	Value	Date	Amount Minted	Value
1913-I	31 million	1.75	1919	60¾ million	.17
1913-D-I	5⅓ million	3.00	1919-D	8 million	2.00
1913-S-I	2 million	5.00	1919-S	7½ million	1.25
1913-II	29¾ million	1.75	1920	63 million	.15
1913-D-II	4¼ million	22.00	1920-D	9½ million	1.50
1913-S-II	1¼ million	45.00	1920-S	9⅔ million	.80
1914	20⅔ million	2.00	1921	10⅔ million	.20
1914-D	4 million	15.00	1921-S	1½ million	6.00
1914-S	3½ million	2.75	1923	35¾ million	.12
1915	21 million	.75	1923-S	6¼ million	.60
1915-D	7½ million	3.25	1924	21⅔ million	.12
1915-S	7½ million	5.25	1924-D	5¼ million	1.00
1916	63½ million	.15	1924-S	1½ million	2.25
1916-D	13⅓ million	2.25	1925	35½ million	.12
1916-S	11¾ million	1.50	1025-D	4½ million	1.75
1917	51½ million	.15	1925-S	6¼ million	.75
1917-D	10 million	2.25	1926	44⅔ million	.10
1917-S	4¼ million	1.75	1926-D	5⅔ million	1.10
1918	32 million	.15	1926-S	970,000	2.75
1918-D	8⅓ million	2.00	1927	38 million	.10
1918-D, 8 over 7		300.00	1927-D	5¾ million	.30
1918-S	4¾ million	1.50			

Date	Amount Minted	Value	Date	Amount Minted	Value
1927-S	3½ million	.60	1935	58¼ million	.10
1928	23½ million	.10	1935-D	12 million	.10
1928-D	6½ million	.12	1935-S	10⅓ million	.10
1928-S	7 million	.15	1936	119 million	.10
1929	36½ million	.10	1936-D	24½ million	.10
1929-D	8⅓ million	.12	1936-S	15 million	.10
1929-S	7¾ million	.12	1937	79½ million	.10
1930	22¾ million	.10	1937-D	17¾ million	.10
1930-S	5½ million	.15	1937-D	3-legged buffalo Used.	50.00
1931-S	1¼ million	1.75	1937-S	5⅔ million	.10
1934	20¼ million	.10	1938-D	7 million	.10
1934-D	7½ million	.10			

Normal type
1938-1942 & 1946 to date

Silver content type with large
Mint Mark on Rev.
1942-1945

Type: Jefferson head.

(From 1938-1942 and 1946-1964, the mint marks are on the Rev. to the right of the building. On the silver content nickels, 1942-1945, the mint marks are much larger and are over the building. From 1968 to date, the mint marks are on the obverse under the date.)

1938	19½ million	.06	1940-D	43½ million	.05
1938-D	5⅓ million	.50	1940-S	39⅔ million	.05
1938-S	4 million	1.00	1941	203¼ million	.05
1939	120⅔ million	.05	1941-D	53½ million	.05
1939-D	3½ million	2.00	1941-S	43½ million	.05
1939-S	6⅔ million	.15	1942	49¾ million	.05
1940	176½ million	.05	1942-D	14 million	.05

Silver content Nickels with large mint mark on reverse.

1942-P	56 million	.40	1944-D	32⅓ million	.40
1942-S	33 million	.40	1944-S	21⅔ million	.40
1943-P	271¼ million	.40	1945-P	119½ million	.40
1943-D	15¼ million	.40	1945-D	37¼ million	.40
1943-S	104 million	.40	1945-S	59 million	.40
1944-P	119¼ million	.40			

Standard composition Nickels.

Date	Amount Minted	Value	Date	Amount Minted	Value
1946	161 million	.05	1947-D	37¾ million	.05
1946-D	45¼ million	.05	1947-S	24¾ million	.06
1946-S	13½ million	.07	1948	89⅓ million	.05
1947	95 million	.05	1948-D	44¾ million	.06

Date	Amount Minted	Value	Date	Amount Minted	Value
1948-S	11⅓ million	.07	1968-D	91¼ million	.05
1949	60⅔ million	.05	1968-S	100⅓ million	.05
1949-D	35¼ million	.05	1969-D	202¾ million	.05
1949-S	9¾ million	.07	1969-S	120¼ million	.05
1950	9¾ million	.15	1970-D	515½ million	.05
1950-D	2⅔ million	6.00	1970-S	238¾ million	.05
1951	28⅔ million	.05	1971	106⁴/₅ million	.05
1951-D	20½ million	.05	1971-D	316 million	.05
1951-S	7¾ million	.35	1971-S	3¼ million proofs	.50
1952	64 million	.05	1972	202 million	.05
1952-D	30⅔ million	.06	1972-D	351⅔ million	.05
1952-S	20½ million	.06	1972-S	3¼ million proofs	.50
1953	46¾ million	.05	1973	384⅓ million	.05
1953-D	59¾ million	.05	1973-D	261⅓ million	.05
1953-S	19¼ million	.06	1973-S	2¾ million proofs	.75
1954	48 million	.05	1974	601¾ million	.05
1954-D	117¼ million	.05	1974-D	277⅓ million	.05
1954-S	29⅓ million	.05	1974-S	2²/₃ million proofs	1.75
1955	8¼ million	.15	1975	181¾ million	.05
1955-D	74½ million	.05	1975-D	402 million	.05
1956	35⅓ million	.05	1975-S	2¾ million proofs	.75
1956-D	67¼ million	.05	1976	367 million	.05
1957	38½ million	.05	1976-D	564 million	.05
1957-D	136¾ million	.05	1976-S	4¼ million	.05
1958	17 million	.05	1977	585⅓ million	.05
1958-D	141¾ million	.05	1977-D	297⅓ million	.05
1959	27¼ million	.05	1977-S	3¼ million proofs	.75
1959-D	160¾ million	.05	1978	391⅓ million	.05
1960	55½ million	.05	1978-D	313 million	.05
1960-D	192½ million	.05	1978-S	3¼ million proofs	.75
1961	73⅔ million	.05	1979	463¼ million	.05
1961-D	229⅓ million	.05	1979-D	325¾ million	.05
1962	97⅓ million	.05	1979-S	3²/₃ million proofs	.75
1962-D	280¼ million	.05	1980	600 million	.05
1963	175¾ million	.05	1980-D	500 million	.05
1963-D	276¾ million	.05	1980-S	3½ million proofs	.75
1964	1 billion	.05	1981	657½ million	.05
1964-D	1¾ billion	.05	1981-D	364¾ million	.05
1965	136 million	.05	1981-S	4 million proofs	.60
1966	156¼ million	.05	1982		.05
1967	107⅓ million	.05	1982-D		.05
			1982-S proof		.60

HALF DIMES

Type: Liberty head with flowing hair.

1794	400.00	1795	400.00

(The combined coinage of 1794 and 1795 was 86,416 pieces. The exact amount
of each year is not known)

Type: Draped bust of Liberty; small eagle on Rev.

Date	Amount Minted	Value	Date	Amount Minted	Value
1796	10,200	**375.00**	1797	44,500	**375.00**

Type: Draped bust of Liberty; large eagle on Rev.

Date	Amount Minted	Value	Date	Amount Minted	Value
1800	24,000	**250.00**	1803	37,800	**250.00**
1801	33,900	**250.00**	1805	15,600	**275.00**
1802	13,000	**1,600.00**			

Type: Bust of Liberty wearing cap.

Date	Amount Minted	Value	Date	Amount Minted	Value
1829	1¼ million	**9.00**	1834	1½ million	**9.00**
1830	1¼ million	**9.00**	1835	2¾ million	**9.00**
1831	1¼ million	**9.00**	1836	2 million	**9.00**
1832	965,000	**9.00**	1837	2¼ million	**9.00**
1833	1⅓ million	**9.00**			

Type: Liberty seated; no stars on Obv.

(The mint mark is under the value on the Rev.)

Date	Amount Minted	Value	Date	Amount Minted	Value
1837	2¼ million	**15.00**	1838-O	Not known	**16.00**

Without arrows at date	With arrows at date
1838-1853 & 1856-1859	1853-1855

Type: Liberty seated; with stars on Obv.

(The mint mark is under the value on the Rev.)

Date	Amount Minted	Value	Date	Amount Minted	Value
1838	2¼ million	4.00	1851-O	860,000	4.25
1839	1 million	4.00	1852	1 million	4.00
1839-O	1 million	4.75	1852-O	260,000	4.75
1840	1⅓ million	4.00	1853 No Arr.	*	6.50
1840-O	935,000	4.75	1853-O No Arr.	*	50.00
1841	1¼ million	4.00	1853 Arr.	13⅓ million	3.75
1841-O	815,000	4.25	1853-O Arr.	2⅓ million	3.75
1842	815,000	4.00	1854	5¾ million	3.75
1842-O	350,000	5.00	1854-O	1½ million	3.75
1843	1¼ million	4.00	1855	1¾ million	3.75
1844	430,000	4.25	1855-O	600,000	4.50
1844-O	220,000	7.00	1856	4¾ million	3.75
1845	1½ million	4.00	1856-O	1 million	4.00
1846	27,000	40.00	1857	7¼ million	3.75
1847	1¼ million	4.00	1857-O	1⅓ million	3.75
1848	668,000	4.00	1858	3½ million	3.75
1848-O	600,000	4.50	1858-O	1⅔ million	3.75
1849	1⅓ million	4.00	1859	340,000	4.00
1849-O	140,000	16.00	1859-O	560,000	4.00
1850	955,000	4.00	*The figures for the No Arrow coinage are		
1850-O	690,000	4.25	included in the figures for the Arrow coin-		
1851	781,000	4.00	age.		

Type: Liberty seated; with "United States of America" on Obv.

(The mint marks are on the Rev., under or within the wreath)

1860	799,000	3.75	1863-S	100,000	6.50
1860-O	1 million	3.75	1864	48,470	100.00
1861	3¼ million	3.75	1864-S	90,000	10.00
1862	1½ million	3.75	1865	13,500	45.00
1863	18,500	30.00	1865-S	120,000	6.00

Date	Amount Minted	Value	Date	Amount Minted	Value
1866	10,700	50.00	1870	536,600	4.00
1866-S	120,000	6.00	1871	1½ million	3.75
1867	8,600	75.00	1871-S	161,000	6.00
1867-S	120,000	6.00	1872	3 million	3.75
1868	85,900	4.75	1872-S	837,000	3.75
1868-S	280,000	4.25	1873	712,600	3.75
1869	208,600	4.00	1873-S	324,000	4.25
1869-S	230,000	4.00			

DIMES

Type: Draped bust of Liberty; small eagle on Rev.

1796	22,100	700.00	1797	25,300	675.00

Type: Draped bust of Liberty; large eagle on Rev.

1798	27,500	300.00	1803	33,000	300.00
1800	21,800	300.00	1804	8,300	400.00
1801	34,600	300.00	1805	120,800	275.00
1802	11,000	300.00	1807	165,000	275.00

Large Size   Reduced Size
1809-1828   1828-1837

Type: Bust of Liberty wearing cap.

1809	44,700	25.00	1811	65,200	17.50

Date	Amount Minted	Value	Date	Amount Minted	Value
1814	421,500	10.00	1829	770,000	8.00
1820	942,600	9.00	1830	510,000	8.00
1821	1¼ million	9.00	1831	771,300	8.00
1822	100,000	30.00	1832	522,500	8.00
1823	440,000	9.50	1833	485,000	8.00
1824	Unknown	10.00	1834	635,000	8.00
1825	510,000	9.00	1835	1⅓ million	8.00
1827	1¼ million	9.00	1836	1¼ million	8.00
1828	125,000	10.00	1837	1 million	8.00

Type: Liberty seated; no stars on Obv.

(The mint mark is under the value on the Rev.)

1837	Unknown	14.00	1838-O	402,400	20.00

Without arrows at date	With arrows at date
1838-1853 & 1856-1860	1853-1855

Type: Liberty seated; with stars on Obv.

(The mint mark is under the value on the Rev.)

Date	Amount Minted	Value	Date	Amount Minted	Value
1838	2 million	5.00	1846	31,300	20.00
1839	1 million	4.25	1847	245,000	4.75
1839-O	1¼ million	4.75	1848	451,500	4.25
1840	1⅓ million	4.25	1849	839,000	3.75
1840-O	1¼ million	4.75	1849-O	300,000	5.25
1841	1⅔ million	3.75	1850	2 million	3.75
1841-O	2 million	3.75	1850-O	510,000	4.25
1842	2 million	3.75	1851	1 million	3.75
1842-O	2 million	4.75	1851-O	400,000	4.75
1843	1⅓ million	3.75	1852	1½ million	3.75
1843-O	150,000	15.00	1852-O	430,000	4.75
1844	72,500	13.00	1853 No. Arr.	12¼ million	12.00
1845	1¾ million	3.75	1853 Arr.		3.75
1845-O	230,000	6.00	1853-O	1 million	4.75

Date	Amount Minted	Value	Date	Amount Minted	Value
1854	4½ million	**3.75**	1858	1½ million	**3.75**
1854-O	1¾ million	**3.75**	1858-O	290,000	**4.75**
1855	2 million	**3.75**	1858-S	60,000	**15.00**
1856	5¾ million	**3.75**	1859	430,000	**3.75**
1856-O	1¼ million	**3.75**	1859-O	480,000	**3.75**
1856-S	70,000	**17.00**	1859-S	60,000	**15.00**
1857	5½ million	**3.75**	1860-S	140,000	**6.00**
1857-O	1½ million	**3.75**			

Without arrows at date
1860-1873 & 1875-1891

With arrows at date
1873-1874

Type: Liberty seated; with "United States of America" on Obv.

(The mint marks are on the Rev., under or within the wreath)

Date	Amount Minted	Value	Date	Amount Minted	Value
1860	607,000	**3.75**	1872-CC	24,000	**75.00**
1860-O	40,000	**175.00**	1873-No Arr.	1¾ million	**3.75**
1861	2 million	**3.75**	1873-Arr.	2¼ million	**5.50**
1861-S	172,500	**8.50**	1873-S	455,000	**9.00**
1862	847,500	**3.75**	1873-CC	18,800	**225.00**
1862-S	180,700	**8.50**	1874	3 million	**5.50**
1863	14,500	**45.00**	1874-S	240,000	**10.00**
1863-S	157,500	**8.50**	1874-CC	10,800	**300.00**
1864	39,000	**50.00**	1875	10⅓ million	**3.75**
1864-S	230,000	**6.00**	1875-S	9 million	**3.75**
1865	10,500	**55.00**	1875-CC	4⅔ million	**3.75**
1865-S	175,000	**6.00**	1876	11½ million	**3.75**
1866	8,700	**60.00**	1876-S	10½ million	**3.75**
1866-S	135,000	**6.00**	1876-CC	8¼ million	**3.75**
1867	6,600	**100.00**	1877	7⅓ million	**3.75**
1867-S	140,000	**6.00**	1877-S	2⅓ million	**3.75**
1868	466,200	**3.75**	1877-CC	7¾ million	**3.75**
1868-S	260,000	**5.00**	1878	1⅔ million	**3.75**
1869	256,600	**3.75**	1878-CC	200,000	**12.00**
1869-S	450,000	**4.75**	1879	15,100	**27.00**
1870	471,500	**3.75**	1880	37,400	**25.00**
1870-S	50,000	**32.00**	1881	25,000	**26.00**
1871	753,600	**3.75**	1882	4 million	**3.75**
1871-S	320,000	**6.00**	1883	7⅔ million	**3.75**
1871-CC	20,100	**150.00**	1884	3⅓ million	**3.75**
1872	2⅓ million	**3.75**	1884-S	565,000	**5.50**
1872-S	190,000	**7.00**	1885	2½ million	**3.75**

Date	Amount Minted	Value	Date	Amount Minted	Value
1885-S	43,700	55.00	1889	7⅓ million	3.75
1886	6⅓ million	3.75	1889-S	972,700	5.00
1886-S	206,500	6.50	1890	10 million	3.75
1887	11¼ million	3.75	1890-S	1½ million	4.00
1887-S	4½ million	3.75	1891	15⅓ million	3.75
1888	5½ million	3.75	1891-O	4½ million	3.75
1888-S	1¾ million	3.75	1891-S	3¼ million	3.75

Type: Liberty head.

(The mint marks are on the Rev., under the wreath)

Date	Amount Minted	Value	Date	Amount Minted	Value
1892	12 million	1.50	1901-S	593,000	17.00
1892-O	3¾ million	2.00	1902	21⅓ million	1.00
1892-S	990,700	12.00	1902-O	4½ million	1.00
1893	3⅓ million	1.50	1902-S	2 million	1.75
1893-O	1¾ million	5.00	1903	19½ million	1.00
1893-S	2½ million	2.25	1903-O	8¼ million	1.00
1894	1⅓ million	3.00	1903-S	613,300	10.00
1894-O	720,000	15.00	1904	14⅔ million	1.00
1894-S	24	—	1904-S	800,000	7.50
1895	690,900	30.00	1905	14½ million	1.00
1895-O	440,000	80.00	1905-O	3½ million	1.00
1895-S	1 million	7.00	1905-S	6¾ million	1.00
1896	2 million	2.50	1906	20 million	1.00
1896-O	610,000	22.00	1906-D	4 million	1.00
1896-S	575,000	20.00	1906-O	2⅔ million	1.50
1897	10¾ million	1.00	1906-S	3¼ million	1.25
1897-O	666,000	20.00	1907	22¼ million	1.00
1897-S	1⅓ million	3.00	1907-D	4 million	1.00
1898	16⅓ million	1.00	1907-O	5 million	1.00
1898-O	2¼ million	1.50	1907-S	3¼ million	1.25
1898-S	1¾ million	1.50	1908	10⅔ million	1.00
1899	19½ million	1.00	1908-D	7½ million	1.00
1899-O	2⅔ million	1.50	1908-O	1¾ million	1.50
1899-S	1¾ million	1.50	1908-S	3¼ million	1.25
1900	17⅔ million	1.00	1909	10¼ million	1.00
1900-O	2 million	2.00	1909-D	954,000	1.50
1900-S	5¼ million	1.00	1909-O	2¼ million	1.00
1901	18¾ million	1.00	1909-S	1 million	1.75
1901-O	5⅔ million	1.00	1910	11½ million	1.50

Date	Amount Minted	Value	Date	Amount Minted	Value
1910-D	3½ million	1.00	1913-S	510,000	3.50
1910-S	1¼ million	1.50	1914	17⅓ million	1.00
1911	19 million	1.00	1914-D	12 million	1.00
1911-D	11¼ million	1.00	1914-S	2 million	1.00
1911-S	3½ million	1.00	1915	5⅔ million	1.00
1912	19⅓ million	1.00	1915-S	960,000	1.25
1912-D	11¾ million	1.00	1916	18½ million	1.00
1912-S	3⅓ million	1.00	1916-S	5¾ million	1.00
1913	19¾ million	1.00			

Type: Mercury head.

(The mint marks are on the bottom of the Rev. to the left of the branches)

Date	Amount Minted	Value	Date	Amount Minted	Value
1916	22¼ million	1.00	1926-S	1½ million	4.25
1916-D	264,000	225.00	1927	28 million	1.00
1916-S	10½ million	1.50	1927-D	4¾ million	1.35
1917	55¼ million	1.00	1927-S	4¾ million	1.00
1917-D	9⅓ million	1.50	1928	19½ million	1.00
1917-S	27⅓ million	1.00	1928-D	4¼ million	1.00
1918	26⅔ million	1.00	1928-S	7⅓ million	1.00
1918-D	22⅔ million	1.00	1929	26 million	1.00
1918-S	19⅓ million	1.00	1929-D	5 million	1.00
1919	35¾ million	1.00	1929-S	4¾ million	1.00
1919-D	10 million	1.35	1930	6¾ million	1.00
1919-S	8¾ million	1.35	1930-S	1¾ million	2.00
1920	59 million	1.00	1931	3¼ million	1.35
1920-D	19¼ million	1.00	1931-D	1¼ million	4.00
1920-S	13¾ million	1.00	1931-S	1¾ million	2.25
1921	1¼ million	13.00	1934	24 million	1.00
1921-D	1 million	19.00	1934-D	6¾ million	1.00
1923	50¼ million	1.00	1935	58¾ million	1.00
1923-S	6½ million	1.35	1935-D	10½ million	1.00
1924	24 million	1.00	1935-S	15¾ million	1.00
1924-D	6¾ million	1.00	1936	87½ million	1.00
1924-S	7 million	1.00	1936-D	16¼ million	1.00
1925	25⅔ million	1.00	1936-S	9¼ million	1.00
1925-D	5 million	2.00	1937	56¾ million	1.00
1925-S	5¾ million	1.00	1937-D	14¼ million	1.00
1926	32¼ million	1.00	1937-S	9¾ million	1.00
1926-D	6¾ million	1.00	1938	22¼ million	1.00

(The valuations in this book are based on the coins being in G-VG condition, unless otherwise noted.)

Date	Amount Minted	Value	Date	Amount Minted	Value
1938-D	5½ million	1.00	1942/1		125.00
1938-S	8 million	1.00	1942-D	60¾ million	1.00
1939	67¾ million	1.00	1942-S	49⅓ million	1.00
1939-D	24⅓ million	1.00	1943	191¾ million	1.00
1939-S	10½ million	1.00	1943-D	72 million	1.00
1940	65⅓ million	1.00	1943-S	60⅓ million	1.00
1940-D	21¼ million	1.00	1944	231½ million	1.00
1940-S	21½ million	1.00	1944-D	62¼ million	1.00
1941	175 million	1.00	1944-S	49½ million	1.00
1941-D	45⅔ million	1.00	1945	159¼ million	1.00
1941-S	43 million	1.00	1945-D	40¼ million	1.00
1942	205½ million	1.00	1945-S	42 million	1.00

Type: Roosevelt head.

(From 1946-1964, the mint marks are on the Rev., at left bottom of torch. From 1968 to date, the mint marks are on the obverse above the date.)

Date	Amount Minted	Value	Date	Amount Minted	Value
1946	255¼ million	1.00	1955-D	14 million	1.00
1946-D	61 million	1.00	1955-S	18½ million	1.00
1946-S	28 million	1.00	1956	108¾ million	1.00
1947	121½ million	1.00	1956-D	108 million	1.00
1947-D	46¾ million	1.00	1957	160¼ million	1.00
1947-S	34¾ million	1.00	1957-D	113⅓ million	1.00
1948	75 million	1.00	1958	32 million	1.00
1948-D	52¾ million	1.00	1958-D	136½ million	1.00
1948-S	35½ million	1.00	1959	85¾ million	1.00
1949	31 million	1.00	1959-D	165 million	1.00
1949-D	26 million	1.00	1960	72 million	1.00
1949-S	13½ million	1.00	1960-D	200¼ million	1.00
1950	50¼ million	1.00	1961	93¾ million	1.00
1950-D	46¾ million	1.00	1961-D	209¼ million	1.00
1950-S	20½ million	1.00	1962	72½ million	1.00
1951	104 million	1.00	1962-D	353 million	1.00
1951-D	52¼ million	1.00	1963	123⅔ million	1.00
1951-S	31⅔ million	1.00	1963-D	421½ million	1.00
1952	92¼ million	1.00	1964	929⅓ million	1.00
1952-D	122 million	1.00	1964-D	1⅓ billion	1.00
1952-S	44½ million	1.00			
1953	53⅔ million	1.00			
1953-D	136½ million	1.00		CLAD COINAGE	
1953-S	39¼ million	1.00	1965	1⅔ billion	.10
1954	114¼ million	1.00	1966	1⅓ billion	.10
1954-D	106⅓ million	1.00	1967	2¼ billion	.10
1954-S	22¾ million	1.00	1968	424½ million	.10
1955	12¾ million	1.00	1968-D	480¾ million	.10

Date	Amount Minted	Value	Date	Amount	Value
1968-S	3 million proofs	.30	1976	568¾ million	.10
1969	145¾ million	.10	1976-D	695¼ million	.10
1969-D	563⅓ million	.10	1976-S	4¼ million proofs	.30
1969-S	3 million proofs	.30	1977	797 million	.10
1970	345½ million	.10	1977-D	376½ million	.10
1970-D	755 million	.10	1977-S	3¼ million proofs	.25
1970-S	2½ million proofs	.30	1978	664 million	.10
1971	162⅔ million	.10	1978-D	282¾ million	.10
1971-D	378 million	.10	1978-S	3¼ million proofs	.40
1971-S	3¼ million proofs	.30	1979	315½ million	.10
1972	431½ million	.10	1979-D	391 million	.10
1972-D	330¼ million	.10	1979-S	3¾ million proofs	.40
1972-S	3¼ million proofs	.30	1980	73.5 million	.10
1973	315⅔ million	.10	1980-D	719⅓ million	.10
1973-D	455 million	.10	1980-S	3½ million proofs	.40
1973-S	2¾ million	.40	1981	676⅔ million	.10
1974	470¼ million	.10	1981-D	712¼ million	.10
1974-D	571 million	.10	1981-S	4 million proofs	.40
1974-S	2⅔ million proofs	.50	1982		.10
1975	585¾ million	.10	1982-D		.10
1975-D	313¾ million	.10	1982-S		.40
1975-S	2¾ million proofs	.50			

20 CENT PIECES

Type: Liberty seated.

(The mint marks are on the Rev., under the eagle)

1875	39,700	25.00	1876-CC	10.000*	———
1875-S	1⅛ million	25.00	1877	510 proofs	1,900.00
1875-CC	133,300	27.00	1878	600 proofs	1,800.00
1876	15,900	30.00	*About a dozen are actually known.		

QUARTERS

Type: Draped bust of Liberty; small eagle on Rev.

1796	5,900	2,000.00

Type: Draped bust of Liberty; large eagle on Rev.

Date	Amount Minted	Value	Date	Amount Minted	Value
1804	6,700	200.00	1806	206,100	90.00
1805	121,400	95.00	1807	220,600	90.00

Type: Bust of Liberty wearing cap; motto over the eagle.

1815	69,200	25.00	1823	17,800	700.00
1818	361,200	25.00	1824	Unknown	25.00
1819	144,000	25.00	1825	168,000	25.00
1820	127,400	25.00	1827	4,000	——
1821	216,900	25.00	1828	102,000	25.00
1822	64,000	25.00			

Type: Bust of Liberty wearing cap; without motto over the eagle.

1831	398,000	22.00	1835	2 million	22.00
1832	320,000	22.00	1836	472,000	22.00
1833	156,000	22.00	1837	252,400	22.00
1834	286,000	22.00	1838	Part of 832,000	22.00

Without arrows or rays
1838-1853 & 1856-1865

With arrows and rays 1853 only
With arrows only, 1854-1855

Type: Liberty seated; without motto over the eagle.

(The mint marks are on the Rev., under the eagle)

Date	Amount Minted	Value	Date	Amount Minted	Value
1838	Part of 832,000	8.00	1854-O	1½ million	4.00
1839	491,100	8.00	1855	2¾ million	4.00
1840	188,127	10.00	1855-O	176,000	25.00
1840-O	425,200	10.00	1855-S	396,400	25.00
1841	120,000	11.00	1856	7¼ million	4.00
1841-O	452,000	6.00	1856-O	968,000	4.00
1842	88,000	30.00	1856-S	286,000	15.00
1842-O	769,000	5.00	1857	9⅔ million	4.00
1843	645,600	5.00	1857-O	1¼ million	4.00
1843-O	968,000	5.00	1857-S	82,000	20.00
1844	421,200	5.00	1858	7⅓ million	4.00
1844-O	740,000	5.00	1858-O	520,000	4.00
1845	922,000	5.00	1858-S	121,000	15.00
1846	510,000	5.00	1859	1⅓ million	4.00
1847	734,000	5.00	1859-O	260,000	5.00
1847-O	368,000	15.00	1859-S	80,000	25.00
1848	146,000	25.00	1860	805,400	4.00
1849	340,000	15.00	1860-O	388,000	4.00
1849-O	Unknown	200.00	1860-S	56,000	35.00
1850	190,800	5.00	1861	4¾ million	4.00
1850-O	412,000	15.00	1861-S	96,000	12.00
1851	160,000	5.00	1862	932,600	4.00
1851-O	88,000	80.00	1862-S	67,000	18.00
1852	177,100	15.00	1863	192,100	10.00
1852-O	96,000	100.00	1864	94,100	15.00
1853 Arr. & Rays	15¼ million	4.00	1864-S	20,000	75.00
1853/3 No Arr.	Part of above	75.00	1865	59,300	22.00
1853-O	1⅓ million	5.00	1865-S	41,000	20.00
1854	12⅓ million	4.00			

**(The valuations in this book are based on the coins
being in G-VG condition, unless otherwise noted.)**

Without arrows at date
1866-1873 & 1875-1891

With arrows at date
1873-1874

Type: Liberty seated; with motto over the eagle.

(The mint marks are on the Rev., under the eagle)

Date	Amount Minted	Value	Date	Amount Minted	Value
1866	17,500	75.00	1876	17¾ million	4.00
1866-S	28,000	30.00	1876-S	8½ million	4.00
1867	20,600	30.00	1876-CC	5 million	4.00
1867-S	48,000	18.00	1877	11 million	4.00
1868	30,000	25.00	1877-S	9 million	4.00
1868-S	96,000	15.00	1877-CC	4¼ million	4.00
1869	16,600	40.00	1878	2¼ million	4:00
1869-S	76,000	14.00	1878-S	140,000	20.00
1870	87,400	12.00	1878-CC	996,000	6.00
1870-CC	8,300	300.00	1879	14,700	40.00
1871	171,200	4.00	1880	15,000	40.00
1871-S	30,900	60.00	1881	13,000	40.00
1871-CC	10,900	250.00	1882	16,300	40.00
1872	182,900	4.00	1883	15,400	40.00
1872-S	83,000	50.00	1884	8,900	45.00
1872-CC	9,100	125.00	1885	14,500	40.00
1873-No Arr.	143,700	5.00	1886	5,900	60.00
1873-CC-No. Arr.	4,000	Rare	1887	10,700	40.00
1873-Arr.	1⅓ million	12.00	1888	10,800	40.00
1873-S-Arr.	156,000	12.00	1888-S	1¼ million	4.00
1873-CC-Arr.	12,500	275.00	1889	12,700	40.00
1874	471,900	12.00	1890	80,600	20.00
1874-S	392,000	12.00	1891	4 million	4.00
1875	4¼ million	4.00	1891-O	68,000	75.00
1875-S	680,000	5.00	1891-S	2¼ million	4.00
1875-CC	140,000	18.00			

The valuations listed in this book closely approximate how much established coin dealers will pay for any material needed in their stock.

Type: Liberty head.

(The mint marks are on the Rev., under the eagle)

Date	Amount Minted	Value	Date	Amount Minted	Value
1892	8¼ million	2.50	1904-O	2½ million	2.50
1892-O	2⅔ million	3.00	1905	5 million	2.50
1892-S	964,100	2.50	1905-O	1¼ million	2.50
1893	5½ million	2.50	1905-S	1¾ million	2.50
1893-O	3½ million	2.50	1906	3⅔ million	2.50
1893-S	1½ million	3.00	1906-D	3⅓ million	2.50
1894	3½ million	2.50	1906-O	2 million	2.50
1894-O	2¾ million	2.50	1907	7¼ million	2.50
1894-S	2⅔ million	2.50	1907-D	2½ million	2.50
1895	4½ million	2.50	1907-O	4½ million	2.50
1895-O	2¾ million	2.75	1907-S	1⅓ million	2.50
1895-S	1¾ million	2.50	1908	4¼ million	2.50
1896	3¾ million	2.50	1908-D	5¾ million	2.50
1896-O	1½ million	3.00	1908-O	6¼ million	2.50
1896-S	188,000	135.00	1908-S	784,000	4.50
1897	8 million	2.50	1909	9¼ million	2.50
1897-O	1½ million	3.00	1909-D	5 million	2.50
1897-S	542,200	4.00	1909-O	712,000	4.50
1898	11 million	2.50	1909-S	1⅓ million	2.50
1898-O	1¾ million	2.75	1910	2¼ million	2.50
1898-S	1 million	2.50	1910-D	1½ million	2.50
1899	12⅔ million	2.50	1911	3¾ million	2.50
1899-O	2⅔ million	2.50	1911-D	933,600	2.50
1899-S	708,000	4.00	1911-S	988,000	2.50
1900	10 million	2.50	1912	4½ million	2.50
1900-O	3½ million	2.50	1912-S	708,000	2.50
1900-S	1¾ million	2.50	1913	484,600	4.50
1901	9 million	2.50	1913-D	1½ million	2.50
1901-O	1⅔ million	4.50	1913-S	40,000	175.00
1901-S	72,700	625.00	1914	6¼ million	2.50
1902	12¼ million	2.50	1914-D	3 million	2.50
1902-O	4¾ million	2.50	1914-S	264,000	7.00
1902-S	1½ million	4.50	1915	3½ million	2.50
1903	9⅔ million	2.50	1915-D	3¾ million	2.50
1903-O	3½ million	2.50	1915-S	704,000	2.50
1903-S	1 million	4.50	1916	1¾ million	2.50
1904	9½ million	2.50	1916-D	6½ million	2.50

Type I. No stars under eagle
1916-1917

Type II. Three stars under eagle
1917-1930

Type: Liberty standing

(The mint marks are on the Obv., above and to left of the date)

Date	Amount Minted	Value	Date	Amount Minted	Value
1916	52,000	700.00	1923-S	1⅓ million	50.00
1917-I	8¾ million	6.00	1924	11 million	8.00
1917-D-I	1½ million	8.00	1924-D	3 million	13.00
1917-S-I	2 million	8.00	1924-S	3 million	8.00
1917-II	14 million	7.00	1925	12¼ million	2.50
1917-D-II	6¼ million	11.00	1926	11¼ million	2.50
1917-S-II	5½ million	11.00	1926-D	1¾ million	2.50
1918	14¼ million	9.00	1926-S	2¾ million	2.50
1918-D	7⅓ million	12.00	1927	12 million	2.50
1918-S	11 million	8.00	1927-D	976,400	4.00
1918-S over 17	——	700.00	1927-S	396,000	6.00
1919	11⅓ million	16.00	1928	6⅓ million	2.50
1919-D	2 million	25.00	1928-D	1⅔ million	2.50
1919-S	1¾ million	25.00	1928-S	2⅔ million	2.50
1920	28 million	7.00	1929	11 million	2.50
1920-D	3½ million	15.00	1929-D	1⅓ million	2.50
1920-S	6⅓ million	8.00	1929-S	1¾ million	2.50
1921	2 million	35.00	1930	5⅔ million	2.50
1923	9¾ million	7.00	1930-S	1⅔ million	2.50

Reg. Obv.
1932-1974

Reg. Rev.
1932-1974

Bicentennial
Obv. — 1976

Bicentennial
Rev. — 1976

Type: Washington head.

(From 1932-1964, the mint marks are on the Rev., under the eagle. From 1968 to date, the mint marks are on the obverse, to the right of Washington's neck.)

Date	Amount Minted	Value	Date	Amount Minted	Value
1932	5½ million	2.50	1935	32½ million	2.50
1932-D	436,800	22.50	1935-D	5¾ million	2.50
1932-S	408,000	20.00	1935-S	5¾ million	2.50
1934	32 million	2.50	1936	41⅓ million	2.50
1934-D	3½ million	2.50	1936-D	5½ million	2.50

Date	Amount Minted	Value	Date	Amount Minted	Value
1936-S	3¾ million	2.50	1959	24⅓ million	2.50
1937	19¾ million	2.50	1959-D	62 million	2.50
1937-D	7¼ million	2.50	1960	30¾ million	2.50
1937-S	1¾ million	2.50	1960-D	63 million	2.50
1938	9½ million	2.50	1961	37 million	2.50
1938-S	2¾ million	2.50	1961-D	80¼ million	2.50
1939	33½ million	2.50	1962	36¼ million	2.50
1939-D	7 million	2.50	1962-D	127½ million	2.50
1939-S	2⅖ million	2.50	1963	74⅓ million	2.50
1940	35¾ million	2.50	1963-D	135¼ million	2.50
1940-D	2¾ million	2.50	1964	560⅓ million	2.50
1940-S	8¼ million	2.50	1964-D	704 million	2.50
1941	79. million	2.50		CLAD COINAGE	
1941-D	16¾ million	2.50	1965	1¾ billion	.25
1941-S	16 million	2.50	1966	821 million	.25
1942	102 million	2.50	1967	1½ billion	.25
1942-D	17½ million	2.50	1968	220¾ million	.25
1942-S	19½ million	2.50	1968-D	101½ million	.25
1943	99¾ million	2.50	1968-S	3 million proofs	.35
1943-D	16 million	2.50	1969	176¼ million	.25
1943-S	21¾ million	2.50	1969-D	114⅓ million	.25
1944	105 million	2.50	1969-S	3 million proofs	.35
1944-D	14⅖ million	2.50	1970	136½ million	.25
1944-S	12⅔ million	2.50	1970-D	417⅓ million	.25
1945	74½ million	2.50	1970-S	2½ million proofs	.35
1945-D	12⅓ million	2.50	1971	109¼ million	.25
1945-S	17 million	2.50	1971-D	258⅔ million	.25
1946	53½ million	2.50	1971-S	3¼ million proofs	.35
1946-D	9 million	2.50	1972	215 million	.25
1946-S	4¼ million	2.50	1972-D	311 million	.25
1947	22⅔ million	2.50	1972-S	3¼ million proofs	.35
1947-D	15⅓ million	2.50	1973	347 million	.25
1947-S	5½ million	2.50	1973-D	233 million	.25
1948	35¼ million	2.50	1973-S	2¾ million proofs	.40
1948-D	16¾ million,	2.50	1974	801½ million	.25
1948-S	16 million	2.50	1974-D	353¼ million	.25
1949	9⅓ million	2.50	1974-S	2⅖ million proofs	.40
1949-D	10 million	2.50	1975	none minted	
1950	25 million	2.50	1976	809¾ million	.25
1950-D	21 million	2.50	1976-D	860 million	.25
1950-S	10⅓ million	2.50	1976-S cupro-nickel, proof, 7 mil.		.35
1951	43½ million	2.50	1976-S	silver	1.25
1951-D	35½ million	2.50	1976-S	silver, proof	2.00
1951-S	9 million	2.50	1977	468½ million	.25
1952	39 million	2.50	1977-D	256½ million	.25
1952-D	49¾ million	2.50	1977-S	3¼ million proofs	.35
1952-S	13¾ million	2.50	1978	521½ million	.25
1953	18¾ million	2.50	1978-D	287¼ million	.25
1953-D	56 million	2.50	1978-S	3¼ million proofs	.40
1953-S	14 million	2.50	1979	515¾ million	.25
1954	54⅔ million	2.50	1979-D	489¾ million	.25
1954-D	46⅓ million	2.50	1979-S	3¾ million proofs	.40
1954-S	11¾ million	2.50	1980	635¾ million	.25
1955	18⅔ million	2.50	1980-D	518⅓ million	.25
1955-D	3¼ million	2.50	1980-S, proof	3½ million proofs	.40
1956	44⅓ million	2.50	1981	601¾ million	.25
1956-D	32⅓ million	2.50	1981-D	575¾ million	.25
1957	46½ million	2.50	1981-S	4 million proofs	.35
1957-D	78 million	2.50	1982		.25
1958	6⅓ million	2.50	1982-D		.25
1958-D	78¼ million	2.50	1982-S		.35

HALF DOLLARS

Type: Liberty head with flowing hair.

Date	Amount Minted	Value	Date	Amount Minted	Value
1794	5,300	**300.00**	1795	317,800	**275.00**

Type: Draped bust of Liberty; small eagle on Rev.

Date	Amount Minted	Value	Date	Amount Minted	Value
1796	Unknown	**7,000.00**	1797	3,900	**7,000.00**

Type: Draped bust of Liberty; large eagle on Rev.

Date	Amount Minted	Value	Date	Amount Minted	Value
1801	30,300	**65.00**	1805	211,700	**40.00**
1802	29,900	**50.00**	1806	839,600	**35.00**
1803	31,700	**45.00**	1807	301,100	**35.00**

(The valuations in this book are based on the coins being in G-VG condition, unless otherwise noted.)

*Type Bust of Liberty wearing cap; motto over eagle;
lettered edge; large size.*

Date	Amount Minted	Value	Date	Amount Minted	Value
1807	750,500	21.00	1823	1⅔ million	17.00
1808	1⅓ million	20.00	1824	3½ million	17.00
1809	1½ million	20.00	1825	3 million	17.00
1810	1¼ million	20.00	1826	4 million	17.00
1811	1¼ million	19.00	1827	5½ million	17.00
1812	1⅔ million	19.00	1828	3 million	17.00
1813	1¼ million	19.00	1829	3¾ million	17.00
1814	1 million	20.00	1830	4¾ million	17.00
1815	47,100	150.00	1831	5¾ million	17.00
1817	1¼ million	18.00	1832	4¾ million	17.00
1818	2 million	18.00	1833	5¼ million	17.00
1819	2¼ million	18.00	1834	6⅓ million	17.00
1820	751,100	21.00	1835	5⅓ million	17.00
1821	1⅓ million	17.00	1836	Part of 6½ million	17.00
1822	1½ million	17.00			

*Type: Bust of Liberty wearing cap; no motto over eagle;
reeded edge; reduced size; value expressed as "50" cents."*

1836	Part of 6½ million	150.00	1837	3⅔ million	20.00

Type: *Same as above; but value is expressed as "Half Dol."*

(The mint marks are on the Obv., over the date)

Date	Amount Minted	Value	Date	Amount Minted	Value
1838	3½ million	**20.00**	1839	Part of 3⅓ million	**20.00**
1838-O	About 20	**Rare**	1839-O	163,000	**40.00**

Without arrows or rays, 1839-1853 & 1856-1866
With arrows and rays, 1853 only
With arrows only, 1854-1855

Type: *Liberty seated; without motto over the eagle.*

(The mint marks are on the Rev., under the eagle)

1839	Part of 3⅓ million	**15.00**	1847-O	2½ million	**9.00**
1840	1½ million	**12.00**	1848	580,000	**9.00**
1840-O	855,100	**12.00**	1848-O	3¼ million	**9.00**
1841	310,000	**15.00**	1849	1¼ million	**9.00**
1841-O	401,000	**9.00**	1849-O	2⅓ million	**9.00**
1842	2 million	**9.00**	1850	227,000	**25.00**
1842-O	957,000	**9.00**	1850-O	2½ million	**9.00**
1843	3¾ million	**9.00**	1851	200,700	**25.00**
1843-O	2¼ million	**9.00**	1851-O	402,000	**9.00**
1844	1¾ million	**9.00**	1852	77,100	**35.00**
1844-O	2 million	**9.00**	1852-O	144,000	**20.00**
1845	589,000	**9.00**	1853-Arr. & Rays 3½ million		**9.00**
1845-O	2 million	**9.00**	1853-O-No Arr. & Rays 1⅓ mil.		**Rare**
1846	2¼ million	**9.00**	1853-O-Arr. & Rays Part of above		**9.00**
1846-O	2⅓ million	**9.00**	1854	3 million	**9.00**
1847	1¼ million	**9.00**	1854-O	5¼ million	**9.00**

Date	Amount Minted	Value	Date	Amount Minted	Value
1855	759,500	9.00	1860	303,700	11.00
1855-O	3⅔ million	9.00	1860-O	1¼ million	9.00
1855-S	129,900	50.00	1860-S	472,000	9.00
1856	938,000	9.00	1861	2¾ million	9.00
1856-O	2⅔ million	9.00	1861-O	2½ million	9.00
1856-S	211,000	12.00	1861-S	939,500	9.00
1857	2 million	9.00	1862	252,300	11.00
1857-O	818,000	9.00	1862-S	1⅓ million	9.00
1857-S	158,000	15.00	1863	503,700	11.00
1858	4¼ million	9.00	1863-S	916,000	9.00
1858-O	7¼ million	9.00	1864	379,600	11.00
1858-S	476,000	10.00	1864-S	658,000	9.00
1859	748,000	9.00	1865	511,900	11.00
1859-O	2¾ million	9.00	1865-S	675,000	9.00
1859-S	566,000	10.00	1866-S	Part of 1 million	30.00

Without arrows at date, 1866-1873 & 1875-1891
With arrows at date, 1873-1874

Type: Liberty seated; with motto over the eagle.

(The mint marks are on the Rev., under the eagle)

Date	Amount Minted	Value	Date	Amount Minted	Value
1866	745,600	8.00	1872-S	580,000	8.00
1866-S	Part of 1 million	8.00	1872-CC	272,000	20.00
1867	424,300	12.00	1873-No Arr.	820,800	8.00
1867-S	1¼ million	8.00	1873-CC-No Arr.	122,500	25.00
1868	378,200	15.00	1873-Arr.	1¾ million	12.00
1868-S	1¼ million	8.00	1873-S-Arr.	228,000	14.00
1869	795,900	8.00	1873-CC-Arr.	214,600	17.00
1869-S	656,000	8.00	1874	2⅓ million	12.00
1870	600,900	8.00	1874-S	394,000	14.00
1870-S	1 million	8.00	1874-CC	59,000	30.00
1870-CC	54,600	100.00	1875	6 million	8.00
1871	1¼ million	8.00	1875-S	3¼ million	8.00
1871-S	2¼ million	8.00	1875-CC	1 million	10.00
1871-CC	139,900	30.00	1876	8½ million	8.00
1872	881,500	8.00	1876-S	4½ million	8.00

Date	Amount Minted	Value	Date	Amount Minted	Value
1876-CC	2 million	8.00	1882	5,500	55.00
1877	8⅓ million	8.00	1883	9,000	50.00
1877-S	5⅓ million	8.00	1884	5,300	55.00
1877-CC	1½ million	8.00	1885	6,100	55.00
1878	1⅓ million	8.00	1886	5,900	55.00
1878-S	12,000	750.00	1887	5,700	55.00
1878-CC	62,000	75.00	1888	12,800	45.00
1879	5,900	55.00	1889	12,700	45.00
1880	9,800	50.00	1890	12,600	45.00
1881	11,000	50.00	1891	200,600	8.00

Type: Liberty Head.

(The mint marks are on the Rev., under the eagle)

Date	Amount Minted	Value	Date	Amount Minted	Value
1892	1 million	7.00	1900	4¾ million	5.00
1892-O	390,000	50.00	1900-O	2¾ million	5.00
1892-S	1 million	52.00	1900-S	2½ million	5.00
1893	1¾ million	6.00	1901	4¼ million	5.00
1893-O	1⅓ million	9.00	1901-O	1 million	5.00
1893-S	740,000	25.00	1901-S	847,000	6.00
1894	1¼ million	5.00	1902	5 million	5.00
1894-O	2¼ million	5.00	1902-O	2½ million	5.00
1894-S	4 million	5.00	1902-S	1½ million	5.00
1895	1¾ million	5.00	1903	2¼ million	5.00
1895-O	1¾ million	5.00	1903-O	2 million	5.00
1895-S	1 million	8.00	1903-S	2 million	5.00
1896	950,800	5.00	1904	3 million	5.00
1896-O	924,000	8.00	1904-O	1 million	6.00
1896-S	1¼ million	25.00	1904-S	553,000	6.00
1897	2½ million	5.00	1905	663,000	5.00
1897-O	632,000	20.00	1905-O	505,000	6.00
1897-S	933,900	55.00	1905-S	2½ million	5.00
1898	3 million	5.00	1906	2½ million	5.00
1898-O	874,000	7.00	1906-D	4 million	5.00
1898-S	2⅓ million	5.00	1906-O	2½ million	5.00
1899	5½ million	5.00	1906-S	1¾ million	5.00
1899-O	1¾ million	5.00	1907	2½ million	5.00
1899-S	1½ million	5.00	1907-D	3¾ million	5.00

Date	Amount Minted	Value	Date	Amount Minted	Value
1907-O	4 million	5.00	1911-S	1¼ million	5.00
1907-S	1¼ million	5.00	1912	1½ million	5.00
1908	1⅓ million	5.00	1912-D	2⅓ million	5.00
1908-D	3¼ million	5.00	1912-S	1⅓ million	5.00
1908-O	5⅓ million	5.00	1913	189,000	9.00
1908-S	1⅔ million	5.00	1913-D	534,000	5.00
1909	2⅓ million	5.00	1913-S	604,000	5.00
1909-O	925,000	5.00	1914	125,000	11.00
1909-S	1¾ million	5.00	1914-S	1 million	5.00
1910	419,000	6.00	1915	138,000	9.00
1910-S	2 million	5.00	1915-D	1¼ million	5.00
1911	1½ million	5.00	1915-S	1⅔ million	5.00
1911-D	695,000	5.00			

Type: Liberty Walking.

(Mint marks: on the coins of 1916 and the early coinage of 1917, the mint marks are on the Obv., under the motto. On the later coinage of 1917 and therafter, the mint marks are on the Rev., to the left of "Half Dollar.")

Date	Amount Minted	Value	Date	Amount Minted	Value
1916	608,000	12.00	1923-S	2¼ million	5.00
1916-D	1 million	10.00	1927-S	2⅓ million	5.00
1916-S	508,000	18.00	1928-S	2 million	5.00
1917	12¼ million	5.00	1929-D	1 million	5.00
1917-D (Obv.)	765,000	6.00	1929-S	2 million	5.00
1917-D (Rev.)	2 million	5.00	1933-S	1¾ million	5.00
1917-S (Obv.)	1 million	6.75	1934	7 million	5.00
1917-S (Rev.)	5½ million	5.00	1934-D	2⅓ million	5.00
1918	6⅔ million	5.00	1934-S	3⅔ million	5.00
1918-D	3¾ million	5.00	1935	9¼ million	5.00
1918-S	10¼ million	5.00	1935-D	3 million	5.00
1919	962,000	6.00	1935-S	3¾ million	5.00
1919-D	1¼ million	5.00	1936	12⅓ million	5.00
1919-S	1½ million	5.00	1936-D	4¼ million	5.00
1920	6⅓ million	5.00	1936-S	4 million	5.00
1920-D	1½ million	5.00	1937	9½ million	5.00
1920-S	4⅔ million	5.00	1937-D	1¾ million	5.00
1921	246,000	35.00	1937-S	2 million	5.00
1921-D	208,000	50.00	1938	4 million	5.00
1921-S	548,000	9.00	1938-D	491,600	14.50

Date	Amount Minted	Value	Date	Amount Minted	Value
1939	6¾ million	5.00	1943-S	13½ million	5.00
1939-D	4¼ million	5.00	1944	28¼ million	5.00
1939-S	2½ million	5.00	1944-D	9¾ million	5.00
1940	9¼ million	5.00	1944-S	9 million	5.00
1940-S	4½ million	5.00	1945	31½ million	5.00
1941	24¼ million	5.00	1945-D	10 million	5.00
1941-D	11¼ million	5.00	1945-S	10¼ million	5.00
1941-S	8 million	5.00	1946	12 million	5.00
1942	47¾ million	5.00	1946-D	2¼ million	5.00
1942-D	11 million	5.00	1946-S	3¾ million	5.00
1942-S	12¾ million	5.00	1947	4 million	5.00
1943	53¼ million	5.00	1947-D	4 million	5.00
1943-D	11⅓ million	5.00			

Type: Franklin head.

(The mint marks are on the Rev., above the Liberty Bell)

Date	Amount Minted	Value	Date	Amount Minted	Value
1948	3 million	5.00	1954-S	5 million	5.00
1948-D	4 million	5.00	1955	3 million	5.00
1949	5¾ million	5.00	1956	4¼ million	5.00
1949-D	4 million	5.00	1957	5 million	5.00
1949-S	3¾ million	5.00	1957-D	20 million	5.00
1950	7¾ million	5.00	1958	4 million	5.00
1950-D	8 million	5.00	1958-D	24 million	5.00
1951	16¾ million	5.00	1959	6¼ million	5.00
1951-D	9½ million	5.00	1959-D	13 million	5.00
1951-S	13⅔ million	5.00	1960	7¾ million	5.00
1952	21¼ million	5.00	1960-D	18¼ million	5.00
1952-D	25⅓ million	5.00	1961	8¼ million	5.00
1952-S	5½ million	5.00	1961-D	20¼ million	5.00
1953	2¾ million	5.00	1962	9¾ million	5.00
1953-D	21 million	5.00	1962-D	35½ million	5.00
1953-S	4¼ million	5.00	1963	22 million	5.00
1954	13½ million	5.00	1963-D	67 million	5.00
1954-D	25½ million	5.00			

Reg. Obv.   Reg. Rev.   Bicentennial   Bicentennial
1964-1974   1964-1974   Obv. — 1976   Rev. — 1976

Type: Kennedy head.

(In 1964 the mint mark is on the Rev., under the eagle's right talon. From 1968 to date, the mint marks are on the obverse, just below the base of Kennedy's neck.)

Date	Amount Minted	Value	Date	Amount Minted	Value
	SILVER		1975	none minted	
1964	277¼ million	5.00	1976	234⅓ million	.50
1964-D	156¼ million	5.00	1976-D	287½ million	.50
	SILVER CLAD		1976-S	cupro-nickel, proof	
1965	65¾ million	1.25		7 million	1.00
1966	109 million	1.25	1976-S	silver	2.00
1967	295 million	1.25	1976-S	silver, proof	4.00
1968-D	247 million	1.25	1977	43½ million	.50
1968-S	3 million proofs	3.00	1977-D	31½ million	.50
1969-D	129¾ million	1.25	1977-S	3¼ million proofs	1.50
1969-S	3 million proofs	3.00	1978	14⅓ million	.50
1970-D	2¼ million	15.00	1978-D	13¾ million	.50
1970-S	2½ million proofs	8.00	1978-S	3¼ million proofs	4.00
	COPPER-NICKEL CLAD		1979	68⅓ million	.50
1971	155¼ million	.50	1979-D	15¾ million	.50
1971-D	302 million	.50	1979-S	3¾ million proofs	3.00
1971-S	3¼ million proofs	3.00	1980	44 million	.50
1972	153 million	.50	1980-D	33½ million	.50
1972-D	141¾ million	.50	1980-S proof	3½ million proofs	3.00
1972-S	3¼ million proofs	3.00	1981	29½ million	.50
1973	65 million	.50	1981-D	27¾ million	.50
1973-D	83 million	.50	1981-S	4 million proofs	3.00
1973-S	2¾ million proofs	3.00	1982		.50
1974	201½ million	50	1982-D		.50
1974-D	79 million	.50	1982-S		3.00
1974-S	2⅔ million proofs	3.00			

SILVER DOLLARS

1794

Type: Head of Liberty with flowing hair.

1,758   **2,000.00** | 1795   Part of 184,000   **1,250.00**

Type: Draped bust of Liberty; with small eagle on Rev.

Date	Amount Minted	Value	Date	Amount Minted	Value
1795	Part of 184,000	650.00	1797	7,800	650.00
1796	72,900	650.00	1798	Part of 327,500	700.00

Type: Draped bust of Liberty; with large eagle on Rev.

1798	Part of 327,500	225.00	1803	66,100	225.00
1799	423,500	225.00	1804	——	——
1800	220,900	225.00	(less than 15 specimens are known of the		
1801	54,500	225.00	1804 Dollar.)		
1802	41,600	225.00			

**Type: Liberty seated; with flying eagle on Rev. — the
Gobrecht design.**

1836	About 1,000	1,000.00	1839	About 300	1,300.00
1838	About 100	3,000.00			

Type: Liberty seated; without motto over the eagle.

(The mint marks are on the Rev., under the eagle)

Date	Amount Minted	Value	Date	Amount Minted	Value
1840	61,000	42.00	1854	33,100	75.00
1841	173,000	40.00	1855	26,000	85.00
1842	184,600	40.00	1856	63,500	70.00
1843	165,100	40.00	1857	94,000	70.00
1844	20,000	75.00	1858	Proof, About 100	2,000.00
1845	24,500	75.00	1859	256,500	40.00
1846	110,600	40.00	1859-O	360,000	40.00
1846-O	59,000	70.00	1859-S	20,000	50.00
1847	140,700	40.00	1860	218,900	40.00
1848	15,000	50.00	1860-O	515,000	40.00
1849	62,600	40.00	1861	78,500	60.00
1850	7,500	90.00	1862	12,100	100.00
1850-O	40,000	40.00	1863	27,700	75.00
1851	1,300	600.00	1864	31,200	75.00
1852	1,100	Rare	1865	47,000	75.00
1853	46,100	45.00			

Type: Liberty seated; with motto over the eagle.

(The mint marks are on the Rev., under the eagle)

Date	Amount Minted	Value	Date	Amount Minted	Value
1866	49,600	50.00	1871	1 million	40.00
1867	60,300	50.00	1871-CC	1,400	300.00
1868	182,700	45.00	1872	1 million	40.00
1869	424,300	40.00	1872-S	9,000	50.00
1870	433,000	40.00	1872-CC	3,100	175.00
1870-S	Unknown	Rare	1873	293,600	40.00
1870-CC	12,500	70.00	1873-CC	2,300	350.00

Type: Liberty head.

(The mint marks are on the Rev., under the eagle)

Date	Amount Minted	Very Fine	Unc	Date	Amount Minted	Very Fine	Unc
1878	10½ million	14.00	35.00	1885-O	9¼ million	14.00	25.00
1878-S	9¾ million	14.00	35.00	1885-S	1½ million	14.00	80.00
1878-CC	2¼ million	18.00	85.00	1885-CC	228,000	100.00	145.00
1879	14¾ million	14.00	27.50	1886	20 million	14.00	25.00
1879-O	3 million	14.00	40.00	1886-O	10¾ million	14.00	225.00
1879-S	9 million	14.00	35.00	1886-S	750,000	17.50	75.00
1879-CC	756,000	40.00	300.00	1887	20¼ million	14.00	25.00
1880	12⅔ million	14.00	27.50	1887-O	11½ million	14.00	35.00
1880-O	5⅓ million	14.00	50.00	1887-S	1¾ million	14.00	47.50
1880-S	9 million	14.00	35.00	1888	19¼ million	14.00	25.00
1880-CC	591,000	35.00	135.00	1888-O	12¼ million	14.00	25.00
1881	9¼ million	14.00	27.50	1888-S	657,000	18.00	80.00
1881-O	5¾ million	14.00	30.00	1889	21¾ million	14.00	25.00
1881-S	12¾ million	14.00	35.00	1889-O	11¾ million	14.00	47.50
1881-CC	296,000	50.00	135.00	1889-S	700,000	17.50	47.50
1882	11 million	14.00	27.50	1889-CC	350,000	200.00	3000.00
1882-O	6 million	14.00	32.50	1890	16¾ million	14.00	32.00
1882-S	9¼ million	14.00	35.00	1890-O	10¾ million	14.00	40.00
1882-CC	1¼ million	18.00	60.00	1890-S	8¼ million	14.00	37.50
1883	12¼ million	14.00	27.50	1890-CC	2⅓ million	18.00	150.00
1883-O	8¼ million	14.00	25.00	1891	8¾ million	14.00	55.00
1883-S	6¼ million	14.00	280.00	1891-O	8 million	14.00	50.00
1883-CC	1¼ million	18.00	60.00	1891-S	5¼ million	14.00	35.00
1884	14 million	14.00	35.00	1891-CC	1⅔ million	18.00	125.00
1884-O	9¾ million	14.00	25.00	1892	1 million	14.00	95.00
1884-S	3¼ million	14.00	900.00	1892-O	2¾ million	14.00	80.00
1884-CC	1¼ million	20.00	60.00	1892-S	1¼ million	19.00	2750.00
1885	17¾ million	14.00	25.00	1892-CC	1⅓ million	21.00	225.00

Date	Amount Minted	Very Fine	Unc	Date	Amount Minted	Very Fine	Unc
1893	379,000	30.00	185.00	1899-O	12¼ million	14.00	27.00
1893-O	300,000	65.00	675.00	1899-S	2½ million	14.00	100.00
1893-S	100,000	1,000.00	12,000.00	1900	8¾ million	14.00	25.00
1893-CC	677,000	95.00	525.00	1900-O	12½ million	14.00	25.00
1894	111,000	200.00	600.00	1900-S	3½ million	14.00	80.00
1894-O	1¾ million	14.00	325.00	1901	7 million	22.50	600.00
1894-S	1¼ million	25.00	225.00	1901-O	13⅓ million	14.00	32.50
1895	880 proofs	—	10,000.00	1901-S	2¼ million	14.00	175.00
1895-O	450,000	75.00	1250.00	1902	8 million	14.00	40.00
1895-S	400,000	85.00	550.00	1902-O	8⅔ million	14.00	25.00
1896	10 million	14.00	25.00	1902-S	1½ million	52.50	150.00
1896-O	5 million	14.00	500.00	1903	4⅔ million	14.00	35.00
1896-S	5 million	22.50	275.00	1903-O	4½ million	115.00	150.00
1897	2¾ million	14.00	27.50	1903-S	1¼ million	25.00	1,000.00
1897-O	4 million	14.00	250.00	1904	2¾ million	14.00	75.00
1897-S	5¾ million	14.00	40.00	1904-O	3¾ million	14.00	25.00
1898	5¾ million	14.00	25.00	1904-S	2⅓ million	32.50	550.00
1898-O	4½ million	14.00	25.00	1921	44⅔ million	14.00	20.00
1898-S	4 million	14.00	95.00	1921-D	20⅓ million	14.00	25.00
1899	331,000	30.00	65.00	1921-S	21⅔ million	14.00	25.00

Type: The Peace Dollar

(The mint marks are on the bottom of the Rev., to left of the eagle's wing)

1921	1 million	20.00	150.00	1926-D	2⅓ million	14.00	45.00
1922	51¾ million	14.00	20.00	1926-S	7 million	14.00	32.00
1922-D	15 million	14.00	22.50	1927	848,000	15.00	80.00
1922-S	17½ million	14.00	22.50	1927-D	1¼ million	14.00	160.00
1923	30¾ million	14.00	20.00	1927-S	866,000	14.00	100.00
1923-D	6¾ million	14.00	22.50	1928	361,000	75.00	160.00
1923-S	19 million	14.00	22.50	1928-S	1⅔ million	14.00	80.00
1924	11¾ million	14.00	22.50	1934	954,000	15.00	65.00
1924-S	1¾ million	14.00	100.00	1934-D	1½ million	14.00	80.00
1925	10¼ million	14.00	22.50	1934-S	1 million	22.50	850.00
1925-S	1⅔ million	14.00	70.00	1935	1½ million	14.00	42.50
1926	2 million	14.00	32.00	1935-S	2 million	14.00	115.00

Reg. Obv.
1971-1974

Reg. Rev.
1971-1974

Bicentennial
Obv. — 1976

Bicentennial
Rev. — 1976

Type: The Eisenhower Dollar

(The mint marks are on the obverse, below Eisenhower's neck)
(The valuations are for uncirculated coins)

Date	Amount Minted	Value	Date	Amount Minted	Value
1971	cupro-nickel, 47¾ million	1.50	1974-S	c.n., proof, 2⅔ million	2.50
1971-D	cupro-nickel, 68½ million	1.50	1974-S	silver, 2 million	8.00
1971-S	silver, 6¾ million	5.00	1974-S	silver, proof, 1⅓ million	13.50
1971-S	silver, proof, 4¼ million	6.00	1975	none minted	
1972	cupro-nickel, 75¾ million	1.50	1976		1.00
1972-D	cupro-nickel, 92½ million	1.50	1976-D		1.00
1972-S	silver, 2¼ million	8.00	1976-S	cupro-nickel, proof	2.50
1972-S	silver, proof, 2 million	8.50	1976-S	silver	5.00
1973	cupro-nickel, 2 million	9.00	1976-S	silver, proof	6.00
1973-D	cupro-nickel, 2 million	9.00	1977	cupro-nickel, 12½ million	1.00
1973-S	cupro-nickel, proof, 2¾ million	3.00	1977-D	cupro-nickel, 33 million	1.00
1973-S	silver, 1¾ million	8.00	1977-S	c.n., proof, 3¼ million	2.00
1973-S	silver, proof, 1 million	65.00	1978	cupro-nickel, 25¾ million	1.00
1974	cupro-nickel, 27⅓ million	1.00	1978-D	cupro-nickel, 23 million	1.00
1974-D	cupro-nickel, 45½ million	1.00	1978-S	c.n., proof, 3 million	4.00

Type: The Anthony Dollar

(The mint marks are on the Obv., to the left of Anthony's neck.
The valuations are for Uncirculated coins.)

Type I—Mint mark is not distinct. Type II—Mint mark is clear

Date	Amount Minted	Value	Date	Amount Minted	Value
1979-P	360¼ million	1.00	1980-S	20½ million	3.00
1979-D	288 million	1.00	1980-S	3½ million proofs	7.00
1979-S	109½ million	1.00	1981-P	3 million	3.00
1979-S Ty. I	3½ million proofs	7.00	1981-D	3¼ million	3.00
1979-S Ty. II	proof	85.00	1981-S	3½ million	3.00
1980-P	27½ million	1.00	1981-S Ty. I	4 million proofs	3.50
1980-D	41½ million	1.00	1981-S Ty. II	proof	25.00

Type: The Trade Dollar

(The mint marks are on the Rev., under the eagle)

Date	Amount Minted	Value	Date	Amount Minted	Value
1873	397,500	30.00	1877-S	9½ million	30.00
1873-S	703,000	30.00	1877-CC	534,000	35.00
1873-CC	124,500	35.00	1878	900 Proofs	2,000.00
1874	987,800	30.00	1878-S	4¼ million	30.00
1874-S	2½ million	30.00	1878-CC	97,000	70.00
1874-CC	1⅓ million	35.00	1879	1,500 Proofs	2,000.00
1875	218,900	40.00	1880	2,000 Proofs	2,000.00
1875-S	4½ million	30.00	1881	1,000 Proofs	2,000.00
1875-CC	1½ million	30.00	1882	1,100 Proofs	2,000.00
1876	456,100	30.00	1883	1,000 Proofs	2,000.00
1876-S	5¼ million	30.00	1884	10 Proofs	——
1876-CC	509,000	35.00	1885	5 Proofs	——
1877	3 million	30.00			

U.S. Silver Commemorative Coins

(All are Half Dollars of standard size and weight except the Isabella Quarter of 1893 and the Lafayette Dollar of 1900)

IMPORTANT NOTE: **The valuations below are for coins in bright, new, uncirculated condition.** Pieces in used or circulated condition are worth less. The amount of coins minted or in existence is shown to the left of the valuation. Because of speculation, the valuations are subject to fluctuation. Coins in exceptionally choice condition are worth considerably more than the prices listed.

COLUMBIAN, 1892-1893

For the World's Columbian Exposition of Chicago, where it was issued on the 400th year of the discovery of America. Head of Columbus. Rev. His flagship, the Santa Maria, over global hemispheres.

1892	950,000 (used 5.50)	15.00
1893	1½ million (used 5.50)	15.00

ISABELLA QUARTER, 1893

For the same event as the Columbian Half Dollar. Crowned head of Queen Isabella of Spain. Rev. Female spinner kneeling.

1893	24,191	300.00

LAFAYETTE DOLLAR, 1900

On the gift by the youth of America to France of an equestrian statue of Lafayette. Conjoined heads of Washington and Lafayette. Rev. The statue as erected in Paris.

1900	36,026	500.00

PANAMA-PACIFIC, 1915

For the Panama-Pacific Exposition in San Francisco on the opening of the Panama Canal. Columbia and child standing at the Golden Gate. Rev. Eagle and shield.

1915-S	27,134	300.00

ILLINOIS, 1918

On the 100th year of Illinois statehood. Head of Lincoln. Rev. Eagle standing to left.

1918	100,058	**62.50**

MAINE, 1920

On the 100th year of Maine statehood. The coat-of-arms of Maine. Rev. Wreath formed of pines and cones.

1920	50,028	**70.00**

PILGRIM, 1920-1921

On the 300th year of the Landing of the Pilgrims at Plymouth Rock. Governor Bradford in Pilgrim dress. Rev. The ship Mayflower.

1920	152,000	**40.00**
1921	20,053	**120.00**

MISSOURI, 1921

On the 100th year of Missouri statehood. Bust of a Missouri pioneer. Rev. Pioneer and Indian standing. The "2 × 4" is located in front of the bust.

1921	15,400	**300.00**
1921 2 × 4	5,000	**325.00**

ALABAMA, 1921

On the 100th year of Alabama statehood. Conjoined heads of Gov. Bibb (1821) and Gov. Kilby (1921). Rev. Eagle. The "2 × 2" is located in back of the busts.

1921	49,000	185.00
1921 2 × 2	5,000	250.00

GRANT, 1922

On the 100th year of his birth. Uniformed bust of the General. Rev. A log cabin in the woods. The * is located on the obverse, over the word, "Grant." Beware of added star.

1922	67,200	65.00
1922*	4,250	500.00

MONROE DOCTRINE, 1923

On the 100th year of Monroe's famous Doctrine. Conjoined heads of Monroe and John Q. Adams. Rev. Allegories depicting North and South America.

1923-S	274,077	35.00

HUGUENOT-WALLOON, 1924

On the 300th year of the settlement of New Netherlands by the Dutch. Conjoined heads of Admiral Coligny and William the Silent. Rev. The ship New Netherlands.

1924	142,080	72.50

LEXINGTON-CONCORD, 1925

On the 150th year of these famous battles of 1775. Armed Minute Man standing. Rev. View of Old Belfry.

1925   162,099   35.00

STONE MOUNTAIN, 1925

On the erection of a Memorial on Stone Mountain to the valor of the Soldier of the South. Gen. "Stonewall" Jackson and Gen. Robert E. Lee on horseback. Rev. Eagle on mountain peak.

1925   1⅓ million (used **6.00**)   **27.50**

CALIFORNIA JUBILEE, 1925

On the 75th year of California Statehood. A "forty-niner" panning gold. Rev. Grizzly bear.

1925-S   86,500   85.00

FORT VANCOUVER, 1925

On the 100th year of the erection of Fort Vancouver. Head of Dr. John McLoughlin, who built the Fort. Rev. Armed pioneer standing before mountain.

1925   14,994   325.00

U.S. INDEPENDENCE, 1926

On the 150th year of the Declaration of Independence. Conjoined heads of Washington and Coolidge. Rev. The Liberty Bell.

1926   141,120   **35.00**

OREGON TRAIL, 1926-1939

In commemoration of this popular but perilous highway to the west. Indian Chief standing before a map of the U.S. Rev. The famous covered wagon of the Trail.

1926	48,030	80.00
1926-S	86,354	80.00
1928	6,028	180.00
1933-D	5,008	300.00
1934-D	7,006	150.00
1936	10,006	100.00
1936-S	5,006	150.00
1937-D	12,008	90.00
1938-P-D-S	6,005 sets, set of 3	375.00
1939-P-D-S	3,004 sets, set of 3	525.00

VERMONT, 1927

On the 150th year both of the Battle of Bennington and of Vermont's independence. Head of Ira Allen. Rev. Vermont mountain lion.

1927   28,142   **175.00**

HAWAII, 1928

On the 150th year of Captain Cook's discovery of the Hawaiian Islands. Bust of the Captain. Rev. Hawaiian Chief in native dress.

1928   10,008   **600.00**

MARYLAND, 1934

On the 300th year of the founding of the Colony. Head of Lord Baltimore, the founder. Rev. The coat-of-arms of Maryland.

1934	25,015	**95.00**

BOONE, 1934-1938

On the 200th year of the birth of Daniel Boone. Head of Boone. Rev. Standing figures of Boone and Indian Chief, Black Fish.

1934	10,007	**70.00**
1935	10,010	
1935-D-S	5,005 pair	set of 3 **200.00**
1935 Small 1934	10,008	**60.00**
1935-D-S Small 1934	2,003 pair	
	set of 2	**700.00**
1936	12,012	
1936-D-S	5,005 pair	set of 3 **200.00**
1937	9,810	
1937-D-S	2,506 pair	set of 3 **700.00**
1938-P-D-S	2,100 sets, set of 3	**700.00**
Type coin (any date)		**60.00**

TEXAS, 1934-1938

On the 100th year of the Independence of Texas. Eagle on a "lone star." Rev. Winged Victory between heads of Sam Houston and Stephen Austin.

1934	61,350	**80.00**
1935	9,934	**80.00**
1935-D	10,007	**80.00**
1935-S	10,008	**80.00**
1936	8,911	**80.00**
1936-D	9,039	**80.00**
1936-S	9,064	**80.00**
1937-P-D-S	6,571 sets, set of 3	**250.00**
1938-P-D-S	3,775 sets, set of 3	**350.00**

ARKANSAS, 1935-1939

On the 100th year of Arkansas Statehood. Liberty head and Indian head conjoined. Rev. Eagle

1935	13,012	**60.00**
1935-D-S	5,505 pair, set of 2	**120.00**
1936-P-D-S	9,660 sets, set of 3	**180.00**
1937-P-D-S	5,505 sets, set of 3	**190.00**
1938-P-D-S	3,155 sets, set of 3	**350.00**
1939-P-D-S	2,104 sets, set of 3	**700.00**

CONNECTICUT, 1935

On the 300th year of the founding of the Colony. The famous Charter Oak Tree. Rev. Eagle.

1935	25,018	**150.00**

HUDSON, 1935

On the 150th year of the founding of the city of Hudson, N.Y. Hudson's ship, the Half Moon. Rev. Neptune on whale, a mermaid in the background.

1935	10,008	**425.00**

SAN DIEGO, 1935-1936

For the California-Pacific International Exposition in San Diego. Seated female and bear. View of Exposition buildings.

1935-S	70,132	**60.00**
1936-D	30,092	**75.00**

OLD SPANISH TRAIL, 1935

On the 400th year of the de Vaca Expedition across the land area of the Gulf of Mexico. Skull of a cow. Rev. Yucca tree and map of the Trail.

1935   10,008   **550.00**

ALBANY, 1936

On the 250th year of Albany's City Charter. Beaver gnawing on maple twigs. Rev. Standing figures of Gov. Dongan, Peter Schuyler and Robert Livingston.

1936   16,887   **190.00**

BRIDGEPORT, 1936

On the 100th year of Bridgeport, Conn. as a city. Head of P. T. Barnum. Rev. Modern style eagle.

1936   25,015   **100.00**

CINCINNATI, 1936

On the 50th year of Cincinnati as a music center. Head of Stephen Foster. Rev. Girl playing harp.

1936   5,005   **200.00**
1936-D   5,005   **200.00**
1936-S   5,006   **200.00**

COLUMBIA, S.C., 1936

On the 150th year of the founding of the city. Standing figure of Justice between the Capitol buildings of 1786 and 1936. Rev. Palmetto tree.

1936	9,007	175.00
1936-D	8,009	175.00
1936-S	8,007	175.00

DELAWARE, 1936

On the 300th year of the Swedish landing in Wilmington. The Swedish ship Kalmar Nyckel. Rev. Old Swede's Church in Wilmington.

1936	25,015	150.00

ELGIN, ILLINOIS, 1936

On the 100th year of the founding of the city. Bearded head of a pioneer. Rev. Four pioneers standing.

1936	25,015	125.00

GETTYSBURG, 1936

For the 75th Anniversary of the Battle of Gettysburg, 1863-1938. Conjoined heads of a Union and Confederate soldier. Rev. Union and Confederate shields.

1936	26,928	200.00

GREAT LAKES, 1936

For the Great Lakes Exposition on the 100th year of Cleveland, Ohio. Head of Moses Cleaveland. Rev. Map of the Great Lakes.

1936   50,030   **60.00**

LONG ISLAND, 1936

On the 300th year of the landing at Jamaica Bay, Long Island by Dutch Settlers. Conjoined heads of a Dutchman and Indian. Rev. Sailing ship.

1936   81,773   **55.00**

LYNCHBURG, 1936

On the 150th year of the city charter given to Lynchburg, Virginia. Head of Senator Carter Glass. Rev. Liberty standing at old courthouse.

1936   20,013   **125.00**

NORFOLK, 1936

On the 200th year of Norfolk, Virginia, becoming a royal borough. Sailing ship as on the city shield. Rev. A large mace.

1936   15,000   **275.00**

RHODE ISLAND, 1936

On the 300th year of the founding of Providence by Roger Williams. Roger Williams in canoe being welcomed by Indian. Rev. Large anchor.

1936	20,013	85.00
1936-D	15,010	85.00
1936-S	15,011	85.00

ROBINSON, 1936

On the 100th year of Arkansas statehood. Head of Senator Joseph T. Robinson. Rev. Eagle. (Identical to the reverse of the Arkansas issues of 1935-1939; the only instance of the same event being commemorated by two different types of Half Dollars.)

1936	25,265	90.00

SAN FRANCISCO, 1936

On the opening of the San Francisco-Oakland Bay Bridge. California grizzly bear. Rev. View of the bridge.

1936-S	71,369	75.00

WISCONSIN, 1936

On the 100th year of the formation of Wisconsin Territory. Forearm holding pickaxe over ore. Rev. Badger on log.

1936	25,015	160.00

YORK COUNTY, ME., 1936

On the 300th year of the founding of York County, Maine. Brown's Garrison at Saco. Rev. The seal of the County.

1936　　　　　25,015　　　　　**150.00**

ANTIETAM, 1937

On the 75th year of the Battle of Antietam. Conjoined heads of the Union's Gen. McClellan and the Confederacy's Gen. Lee. Rev. Burnside Bridge for which the battle was fought.

1937　　　　　18,028　　　　　**250.00**

ROANOKE, 1937

On the 350th year of the colonization of Roanoke Island by Sir Walter Raleigh; also on the birth of Virginia Dare in 1587, the first white child born in America. Bust of Sir Walter Raleigh. Rev. Mother holding Virginia Dare.

1937　　　　　29,030　　　　　**120.00**

NEW ROCHELLE, 1938

On the 250th year of the founding of New Rochelle, New York, by the Huguenots. Lord Pell holding fatted calf. Rev. Fleur-de-lis.

1938　　　　　15,266　　　　　**275.00**

IOWA, 1946

On the 100th year of Iowa Statehood. Eagle on scroll. Rev. The old Capitol Statehouse at Iowa City.

1946	100,057	**60.00**

B.T.W., 1946-1951

In honor of this great black leader and educator. Head of Booker T. Washington. Rev. View of the log cabin of his birth and of the Hall of Fame where he is inscribed.

1946	1 million	**10.00**
1946-D	200,113	**10.00**
1946S	500,279	**10.00**
1947-P-D-S	100,017 sets, set of 3	**50.00**
1948-P-D-S	8,005 sets, set of 3	**100.00**
1949-P-D-S	6,004 sets, set of 3	**145.00**
1950-P-D-S	6,004 sets, set of 3	**125.00**
1950-S	403,996	**10.00**
1951	503,078	**10.00**
1951-P-D-S	7,004 sets, set of 3	**80.00**

G.W.C.-B.T.W., 1951-1954

In honor of the famous black leaders, George Washington Carver and Booker T. Washington. Their conjoined heads. Rev. Map of the United States.

1951	100,014	**10.00**
1951-P-D-S	10,004 sets, set of 3	**70.00**
1952	2 million	**10.00**
1952-P-D-S	8,000 sets, set of 3	**85.00**
1953-P-D-S	8,000 sets, set of 3	**115.00**
1953-S	100,000	**10.00**
1954-P-D-S	12,000 sets, set of 3	**70.00**
1954-S	110,000	**10.00**

U.S. Gold Commemorative Coins

IMPORTANT NOTE: The valuations below are for coins in bright, new, uncirculated condition. Pieces in used or circulated condition are worth less. The amount of coins minted or in existence is shown to the left of the valuation.

LOUISIANA PURCHASE ISSUE, 1903

Two types of Gold Dollars were struck to commemorate the Centennial of the Louisiana Purchase. The same reverse appears on both.

1 Dollar 1903	Head of Jefferson	17,375	475.00
1 Dollar 1903	Head of McKinley	17,375	475.00

LEWIS AND CLARK ISSUE, 1904-1905

Two dates of a Gold Dollar were struck to commemorate the Centennial of the Lewis and Clark Expedition. The head of Lewis appears on one side and that of Clark on the other.

1 Dollar 1904	9,997	1,000.00
1 Dollar 1905	10,000	1,000.00

PANAMA PACIFIC ISSUE, 1915

Four types of gold coins were struck for the Panama-Pacific Exposition commemorating the opening of the Panama Canal.

1 Dollar 1915-S	Head of worker	25,000	550.00

2½ Dollars 1915-S	Columbia on hippocampus	6,749	**1,400.00**

50 Dollars 1915-S, round	Head of Minerva	483	**25,000.00**
50 Dollars 1915-S, octagonal	Head of Minerva	645	**19,000.00**

McKINLEY MEMORIAL ISSUE, 1916-1917

Two dates of a Gold Dollar were struck to commemorate the erection of the McKinley Memorial at Niles, Ohio. The obverse shows his head, and the reverse the memorial building.

1 Dollar 1916		9,977	**500.00**
1 Dollar 1917		10,000	**525.00**

GRANT CENTENNIAL ISSUE, 1922

Two varieties of a Gold Dollar were struck to commemorate the 100th year of Grant's birth. His head appears on the obverse and a log cabin on the reverse. The star is located on the obverse, over the word, "Grant."

1 Dollar 1922	5,000	800.00
1 Dollar 1922 with star	5,000	900.00

U.S. INDEPENDENCE ISSUE, 1926

A 2½ Dollar gold piece was struck to commemorate the Sesquicentennial (150th year) of the Declaration of Independence. The obverse shows Liberty standing; the reverse a view of Independence Hall in Philadelphia.

2½ Dollars 1926	46,019	**400.00**

United States Gold Coins

(The valuations are for coins in choice VF-EF condition. Americans traveling abroad are cautioned to beware of counterfeit U.S. gold pieces in all denominations, which are being produced in many parts of Europe and Asia.)

1 DOLLAR GOLD PIECES

Type: *Liberty head with coronet. Small size.*

(The mint marks are on the Rev., under the wreath)

Date	Amount Minted	Value	Date	Amount Minted	Value
1849	688,600	100.00	1852	2 million	100.00
1849-O	215,000	100.00	1852-O	140,000	100.00
1849-C	11,600	150.00	1852-C	9,400	125.00
1849-D	21,600	150.00	1852-D	6,400	130.00
1850	482,000	100.00	1853	4 million	100.00
1850-O	14,000	100.00	1853-O	290,000	100.00
1850-C	7,000	125.00	1853-C	11,500	115.00
1850-D	8,400	125.00	1853-D	6,600	125.00
1851	3⅓ million	100.00	1854	Part of 1⅔ million	100.00
1851-O	290,000	100.00	1854-D	2,900	175.00
1851-C	41,300	115.00	1854-S	14,600	100.00
1851-D	9,900	125.00			

Type: Small Liberty head with feather head-dress.
Large size.

(The mint marks are on the Rev., under the wreath)

Date	Amount Minted	Value	Date	Amount Minted	Value
1854	Part of 1⅔ million	190.00	1855-C	9,800	240.00
1855	758,300	190.00	1855-D	1,800	1,000.00
1855-O	55,000	190.00	1856-S	24,600	190.00

Type: Large Liberty head with feather head-dress.
Large size.

(The mint marks are on the Rev., under the wreath)

Date	Amount Minted	Value	Date	Amount Minted	Value
1856	1¾ million	100.00	1868	10,500	125.00
1856-D	1,500	1500.00	1869	5,900	125.00
1857	774,800	100.00	1870	6,300	125.00
1857-C	13,300	125.00	1870-S	3,000	200.00
1857-D	3,500	200.00	1871	3,900	125.00
1857-S	10,000	125.00	1872	3,500	125.00
1858	118,000	100.00	1873	125,100	100.00
1858-D	3,500	300.00	1874	198,800	100.00
1858-S	10,000	125.00	1875	400	1500.00
1859	168,200	100.00	1876	3,200	125.00
1859-C	5,200	200.00	1877	3,900	125.00
1859-D	5,000	400.00	1878	3,000	125.00
1859-S	15,000	125.00	1879	3,000	125.00
1860	36,700	100.00	1880	1,600	125.00
1860-D	1,600	1400.00	1881	7,700	100.00
1860-S	13,000	125.00	1882	5,000	100.00
1861	527,500	100.00	1883	10,800	100.00
1861-D	Unknown	2000.00	1884	6,200	100.00
1862	1⅓ million	100.00	1885	12,200	100.00
1863	6,200	150.00	1886	6,000	100.00
1864	5,900	150.00	1887	8,500	100.00
1865	3,700	150.00	1888	16,100	100.00
1866	7,200	125.00	1889	30,700	100.00
1867	5,200	125.00			

2½ DOLLAR GOLD PIECES (QUARTER EAGLES)

Type: Liberty head; without stars on Obv.

Date	Amount Minted	Value	Date	Amount Minted	Value
1796	Part of 1,400	5,000.00			

Type: Liberty head; with stars on Obv.

Date	Amount Minted	Value	Date	Amount Minted	Value
1796	Part of 1,400	4,000.00	1804	3,300	1,000.00
1797	1,700	3,000.00	1805	1,800	1,000.00
1798	600	1,200.00	1806	1,600	1,100.00
1802 over 1	2,600	1,000.00	1807	6,800	900.00

Type: Draped bust of Liberty with round cap.

Date	Amount Minted	Value	
1808	2,700	4,000.00	

Type: Undraped head of Liberty with round cap; with motto over eagle.

Date	Amount Minted	Value	Date	Amount Minted	Value
1821	6,400	1,500.00	1824 over 21	2,600	1,500.00

2½ Dollar Gold Pieces (continued) 111

Date	Amount Minted	Value	Date	Amount Minted	Value
1825	4,400	1,500.00	1831	4,500	1,000.00
1826 over 25	800	2,000.00	1832	4,400	1,000.00
1827	2,800	1,500.00	1833	4,200	1,000.00
1829	3,400	1,000.00	1834	4,000	3,000.00
1830	4,500	1,000.00			

Type: Liberty head with ribbon; without motto over eagle.

(The mint marks are on the Obv., over the date)

Date	Amount Minted	Value	Date	Amount Minted	Value
1834	112,200	200.00	1838-C	7,900	275.00
1835	131,400	200.00	1839	27,000	200.00
1836	548,000	200.00	1839-O	17,800	225.00
1837	45,100	200.00	1839-C	18,200	250.00
1838	47,000	200.00	1839-D	13,700	275.00

Type: Liberty head with coronet.

(The mint marks are on the Rev., under the eagle. The "CAL" on the 1848 is over the eagle and represents gold mined in California)

Date	Amount Minted	Value	Date	Amount Minted	Value
1840	18,900	150.00	1844	6,800	150.00
1840-O	26,200	150.00	1844-C	11,600	160.00
1840-C	12,800	275.00	1844-D	17,300	160.00
1840-D	3,500	325.00	1845	91,100	150.00
1841	A few proofs	—	1845-O	4,000	250.00
1841-C	10,300	300.00	1845-D	19,500	160.00
1841-D	4,200	325.00	1846	21,600	150.00
1842	2,800	300.00	1846-O	66,000	150.00
1842-O	19,800	150.00	1846-C	4,800	250.00
1842-C	6,700	300.00	1846-D	19,300	160.00
1842-D	4,600	325.00	1847	29,800	150.00
1843	100,500	150.00	1847-O	124,000	150.00
1843-O	368,000	150.00	1847-C	23,200	160.00
1843-C	26,100	300.00	1847-D	15,800	160.00
1843-D	36,200	300.00	1848	7,500	300.00

2½ Dollar Gold Pieces (continued)

Date	Amount Minted	Value	Date	Amount Minted	Value
1848-CAL	1,400	2500.00	1862-S	8,000	140.00
1848-C	16,800	200.00	1863	30 proofs	——
1848-D	13,800	250.00	1863-S	10,800	140.00
1849	23,300	140.00	1864	2,900	375.00
1849-C	10,200	200.00	1865	1,500	375.00
1849-D	10,900	200.00	1865-S	23,400	140.00
1850	252,900	140.00	1866	3,100	175.00
1850-O	84,000	140.00	1866-S	39,000	140.00
1850-C	9,100	200.00	1867	3,200	175.00
1850-D	12,100	200.00	1867-S	28,000	140.00
1851	1⅓ million	140.00	1868	3,600	165.00
1851-O	148,000	140.00	1868-S	34,000	140.00
1851-C	14,900	200.00	1869	4,300	150.00
1851-D	11,300	200.00	1869-S	29,500	140.00
1852	1¼ million	140.00	1870	4,600	150.00
1852-O	142,000	140.00	1870-S	16,000	140.00
1852-C	9,800	200.00	1871	5,300	150.00
1852-D	4,000	275.00	1871-S	22,000	140.00
1853	1⅓ million	140.00	1872	3,000	165.00
1853-D	3,200	275.00	1872-S	18,000	140.00
1854	596,300	140.00	1873	178,000	140.00
1854-O	153,000	140.00	1873-S	27,000	140.00
1854-C	7,300	200.00	1874	3,900	160.00
1854-D	1,800	1000.00	1875	420	1000.00
1854-S	246	10000.00	1875-S	11,600	140.00
1855	235,500	140.00	1876	4,200	150.00
1855-C	3,700	375.00	1876-S	5,000	140.00
1855-D	1,100	900.00	1877	1,700	200.00
1856	384,200	150.00	1877-S	35,400	140.00
1856-O	21,100	140.00	1878	286,300	140.00
1856-C	7,900	200.00	1878-S	178,000	140.00
1856-D	874	1500.00	1879	89,000	140.00
1856-S	71,100	140.00	1879-S	43,500	140.00
1857	214,100	140.00	1880	3,000	150.00
1857-O	34,000	140.00	1881	680	300.00
1857-D	2,400	250.00	1882	4,000	140.00
1857-S	68,000	140.00	1883	2,000	165.00
1858	47,400	140.00	1884	2,000	165.00
1858-C	9,100	175.00	1885	887	300.00
1859	39,400	140.00	1886	4,100	150.00
1859-D	2,200	250.00	1887	6,300	140.00
1859-S	15,200	140.00	1888	16,100	140.00
1860	22,700	140.00	1889	17,600	140.00
1860-C	7,500	175.00	1890	8,800	140.00
1860-S	35,600	140.00	1891	11,000	140.00
1861	1¼ million	140.00	1892	2,500	140.00
1861-S	24,000	140.00	1893	30,100	140.00
1862	112,400	140.00	1894	4,100	150.00

Date	Amount Minted	Value	Date	Amount Minted	Value
1895	6,100	140.00	1902	133,700	140.00
1896	19,200	140.00	1903	201,300	140.00
1897	29,900	140.00	1904	161,000	140.00
1898	24,200	140.00	1905	217,900	140.00
1899	27,300	140.00	1906	176,500	140.00
1900	67,200	140.00	1907	336,400	140.00
1901	91,300	140.00			

Type: Indian Head

(The mint marks are on the Rev., to the left of the value)

Date	Amount Minted	Value	Date	Amount Minted	Value
1908	565,000	125.00	1914-D	448,000	125.00
1909	441,900	125.00	1915	606,100	125.00
1910	492,700	125.00	1925-D	578,000	125.00
1911	704,200	125.00	1926	446,000	125.00
1911-D	55,700	650.00	1927	388,000	125.00
1912	616,200	125.00	1928	416,000	125.00
1913	722,200	125.00	1929	532,000	125.00
1914	240,100	125.00			

3 DOLLAR GOLD PIECES

Type: Liberty head with feather head-dress

(The mint marks are on the Rev., under the wreath)

Date	Amount Minted	Value	Date	Amount Minted	Value
1854	138,600	375.00	1856-S	34,500	375.00
1854-O	24,000	375.00	1857	20,900	375.00
1854-D	1,100	1500.00	1857-S	14,000	375.00
1855	50,600	375.00	1858	2,100	400.00
1855-S	6,600	375.00	1859	15,600	375.00
1856	26,000	375.00	1860	7,200	375.00

Date	Amount Minted	Value	Date	Amount Minted	Value
1860-S	7,000	375.00	1875	About 50 proofs	——
1861	6,100	375.00	1876	About 50 proofs	——
1862	5,800	375.00	1877	1,500	475.00
1863	5,000	375.00	1878	82,300	575.00
1864	2,700	500.00	1879	3,000	475.00
1865	1,200	600.00	1880	1,000	400.00
1866	4,000	375.00	1881	550	475.00
1867	2,600	375.00	1882	1,500	400.00
1868	4,900	375.00	1883	900	400.00
1869	2,500	375.00	1884	1,100	400.00
1870	3,500	375.00	1885	900	400.00
1870-S	2	——	1886	1,100	400.00
1871	1,300	475.00	1887	6,200	375.00
1872	2,000	375.00	1888	5,300	375.00
1873	About 100 proofs	——	1889	2,400	375.00
1874	41,800	375.00			

4 DOLLAR GOLD PIECES (STELLAS)

Type: Liberty head with flowing hair.

1879   415 proofs   **20,000.00** | 1880   15 proofs   ——

Type: Liberty head with coiled hair.

1879   10 proofs   —— | 1880   10 proofs   ——

5 DOLLAR GOLD PIECES (HALF EAGLES)

Type: Liberty head; with small eagle on Rev.

Date	Amount Minted	Value	Date	Amount Minted	Value
1795	Part of 8,700	2,000.00	1797	Part of 6,400	2,500.00
1796	3,400	2,000.00	1798	Part of 24,900	——

Type: Liberty head to right; with large eagle on Rev.

Date	Amount Minted	Value	Date	Amount Minted	Value
1795	Part of 8,700	2,500.00	1803	33,500	600.00
1797	Part of 6,400	2,000.00	1804	30,500	600.00
1798	Part of 24,900	600.00	1805	33,200	600.00
1799	7,500	600.00	1806	64,100	600.00
1800	11,600	600.00	1807	Part of 84,100	600.00
1802	53,200	600.00			

Type: Draped bust of Liberty to left with round cap.

Date	Amount Minted	Value	Date	Amount Minted	Value
1807	Part of 84,100	650.00	1810	100,300	600.00
1808	55,600	600.00	1811	99,600	600.00
1809	33,900	600.00	1812	58,100	600.00

Type: Liberty head with round cap; with motto over eagle.

Date	Amount Minted	Value	Date	Amount Minted	Value
1813	95,400	600.00	1825	29,100	1,500.00
1814	15,500	800.00	1826	18,100	1,600.00
1815	635	——	1827	24,900	——
1818	48,600	800.00	1828	28,000	——
1819	51,700	——	1829	57,400	——
1820	263,800	800.00	1830	126,400	1,000.00
1821	34,600	1,500.00	1831	140,600	1,000.00
1822	17,800	——	1832	157,500	1,500.00
1823	14,500	1,000.00	1833	193,600	1,000.00
1824	17,300	3,500.00	1834	Part of 732,200	1,000.00

Type: Liberty head with ribbon; without motto over eagle.

(The mint marks are on the Obv., over the date)

Date	Amount Minted	Value	Date	Amount Minted	Value
1834	Part of 732,200	175.00	1838	286,600	175.00
1835	371,500	175.00	1838-C	12,900	500.00
1836	553,100	175.00	1838-D	20,600	500.00
1837	207,100	175.00			

Type: Liberty head with coronet; without motto over eagle.

(The mint marks are on the Rev., under the eagle)

Date	Amount Minted	Value	Date	Amount Minted	Value
1839	118,100	130.00	1852-D	91,500	175.00
1839-C	23,500	175.00	1853	305,800	130.00
1839-D	18,900	175.00	1853-C	65,600	175.00
1840	137,400	130.00	1853-D	89,700	175.00
1840-O	30,400	130.00	1854	160,700	130.00
1840-C	19,000	150.00	1854-O	46,000	130.00
1840-D	22,900	150.00	1854-C	39,300	150.00
1841	15,800	130.00	1854-D	56,400	150.00
1841-O	8,300	——	1854-S	268	——
1841-C	21,500	150.00	1855	117,100	130.00
1841-D	30,500	150.00	1855-O	11,100	175.00
1842	27,600	130.00	1855-C	39,800	160.00
1842-O	16,400	150.00	1855-D	22,400	160.00
1842-C	27,500	150.00	1855-S	61,000	130.00
1842-D	59,600	150.00	1856	198,000	130.00
1843	611,200	130.00	1856-O	10,000	200.00
1843-O	101,100	130.00	1856-C	28,500	160.00
1843-C	44,400	150.00	1856-D	19,800	160.00
1843-D	98,500	150.00	1856-S	105,100	130.00
1844	340,300	130.00	1857	98,200	130.00
1844-O	364,600	130.00	1857-O	13,000	130.00
1844-C	23,600	150.00	1857-C	31,400	160.00
1844-D	89,000	150.00	1857-D	17,000	160.00
1845	417,100	130.00	1857-S	87,000	130.00
1845-O	41,000	130.00	1858	15,100	150.00
1845-D	90,600	150.00	1858-C	38,900	150.00
1846	395,900	130.00	1858-D	15,400	175.00
1846-O	58,000	130.00	1858-S	18,600	130.00
1846-C	13,000	175.00	1859	16,800	130.00
1846-D	80,300	150.00	1859-C	31,800	175.00
1847	916,000	130.00	1859-D	10,400	190.00
1847-O	12,000	150.00	1859-S	13,200	130.00
1847-C	84,200	175.00	1860	19,800	130.00
1847-D	64,400	175.00	1860-C	14,800	175.00
1848	260,800	130.00	1860-D	14,600	175.00
1848-C	64,500	175.00	1860-S	21,200	130.00
1848-D	47,500	175.00	1861	639,900	130.00
1849	133,100	130.00	1861-C	6,900	400.00
1849-C	64,800	175.00	1861-D	1,600	1,500.00
1849-D	39,000	175.00	1861-S	18,000	130.00
1850	64,500	130.00	1862	4,500	175.00
1850-C	63,600	175.00	1862-S	9,500	130.00
1850-D	43,900	175.00	1863	2,500	250.00
1851	377,500	130.00	1863-S	17,000	130.00
1851-O	41,000	130.00	1864	4,200	200.00
1851-C	49,200	175.00	1864-S	3,900	500.00
1851-D	62,700	175.00	1865	1,300	400.00
1852	573,900	130.00	1865-S	27,600	130.00
1852-C	72,600	175.00	1866-S	Part of 43,900	150.00

Type: Liberty head with coronet; with motto over eagle.

(The mint marks are on the Rev., under the eagle)

Date	Amount Minted	Value	Date	Amount Minted	Value
1866	6,700	175.00	1879-CC	17,300	150.00
1866-S	Part of 43,900	150.00	1880	3¼ million	130.00
1867	6,900	150.00	1880-S	1⅓ million	130.00
1867-S	29,000	130.00	1880-CC	51,000	150.00
1868	5,700	175.00	1881	5⅔ million	130.00
1868-S	52,000	130.00	1881-S	969,000	130.00
1869	1,800	225.00	1881-CC	13,900	150.00
1869-S	31,000	130.00	1882	2½ million	130.00
1870	4,000	150.00	1882-S	970,000	130.00
1870-S	17,000	140.00	1882-CC	82,800	150.00
1870-CC	7,700	800.00	1883	233,400	130.00
1871	3,200	175.00	1883-S	83,200	130.00
1871-S	25,000	130.00	1883-CC	13,000	150.00
1871-CC	20,800	190.00	1884	191,000	130.00
1872	1,700	250.00	1884-S	177,000	130.00
1872-S	36,400	130.00	1884-CC	16,400	150.00
1872-CC	17,000	190.00	1885	601,500	130.00
1873	112,500	130.00	1885-S	1¼ million	130.00
1873-S	31,000	130.00	1886	388,400	130.00
1873-CC	7,400	250.00	1886-S	3¼ million	130.00
1874	3,500	190.00	1887	87 proofs	——
1874-S	16,000	130.00	1887-S	2 million	130.00
1874-CC	21,200	160.00	1888	18,300	130.00
1875	220	——	1888-S	293,900	130.00
1875-S	9,000	150.00	1889	7,600	175.00
1875-CC	11,800	190.00	1890	4,300	190.00
1876	1,500	225.00	1890-CC	53,800	150.00
1876-S	4,000	150.00	1891	61,400	130.00
1876-CC	6,900	225.00	1891-CC	208,000	150.00
1877	1,200	250.00	1892	753,600	130.00
1877-S	26,700	130.00	1892-O	10,000	250.00
1877-CC	8,700	200.00	1892-S	298,400	130.00
1878	131,700	130.00	1892-CC	83,000	150.00
1878-S	144,700	130.00	1893	1½ million	130.00
1878-CC	9,100	600.00	1893-O	110,000	130.00
1879	301,900	130.00	1893-S	224,000	130.00
1879-S	426,200	130.00	1893-CC	60,000	150.00

Date	Amount Minted	Value	Date	Amount Minted	Value
1894	958,000	130.00	1901-S	3⅔ million	130.00
1894-O	16,600	150.00	1902	172,600	130.00
1894-S	55,900	130.00	1902-S	939,000	130.00
1895	1⅓ million	130.00	1903	227,000	130.00
1895-S	112,000	130.00	1903-S	1¾ million	130.00
1896	59,100	130.00	1904	392,100	130.00
1896-S	155,400	130.00	1904-S	97,000	130.00
1897	867,900	130.00	1905	302,300	130.00
1897-S	354,000	130.00	1905-S	880,700	130.00
1898	633,500	130.00	1906	348,800	130.00
1898-S	1⅓ million	130.00	1906-S	598,000	130.00
1899	1¾ million	130.00	1906-D	320,000	130.00
1899-S	1½ million	130.00	1907	626,200	130.00
1900	1⅓ million	130.00	1907-D	888,000	130.00
1900-S	329,000	130.00	1908	421,900	130.00
1901	616,000	130.00			

Type: Indian head.

(The mint marks are on the Rev., to the left of the value)

Date	Amount Minted	Value	Date	Amount Minted	Value
1908	578,000	175.00	1911-S	1½ million	175.00
1908-D	148,000	175.00	1912	790,100	175.00
1908-S	82,000	235.00	1912-S	392,000	175.00
1909	627,100	175.00	1913	916,100	175.00
1909-O	34,200	650.00	1913-S	408,000	175.00
1909-D	3½ million	175.00	1914	247,100	175.00
1909-S	297,200	175.00	1914-D	247,000	175.00
1910	604,200	175.00	1914-S	263,000	175.00
1910-D	193,600	175.00	1915	588,100	175.00
1910-S	770,200	175.00	1915-S	164,000	175.00
1911	915,100	175.00	1916-S	240,000	175.00
1911-D	72,500	250.00	1929	662,000	2,000.00

The valuations listed in this book closely approximate how much established coin dealers will pay for any material needed in their stock.

10 DOLLAR GOLD PIECES (EAGLES)

Type: Liberty head; with small eagle on Rev.

Date	Amount Minted	Value	Date	Amount Minted	Value
1795	2,800	3,000.00	1797	Part of 9,200	3,000.00
1796	6,100	3,000.00			

Type: Liberty head; with large eagle on Rev.

Date	Amount Minted	Value	Date	Amount Minted	Value
1797	Part of 9,200	1,300.00	1801	29,300	1,000.00
1798	8,000	2,000.00	1803	9,000	1,100.00
1799	17,500	1,000.00	1804	9,800	1,300.00
1800	26,000	1,100.00			

Type: Liberty head; without motto on Rev.

(The mint marks are on the Rev., under the eagle)

Date	Amount Minted	Value	Date	Amount Minted	Value
1838	7,200	400.00	1840	47,300	225.00
1839	38,200	300.00	1841	63,100	225.00

Date	Amount Minted	Value	Date	Amount Minted	Value
1841-O	2,500	250.00	1855-O	18,000	225.00
1842	81,500	225.00	1855-S	9,000	250.00
1842-O	27,400	225.00	1856	60,500	225.00
1843	75,500	225.00	1856-O	14,500	225.00
1843-O	175,200	225.00	1856-S	68,000	225.00
1844	6,400	250.00	1857	16,600	225.00
1844-O	118,700	225.00	1857-O	5,500	250.00
1845	26,200	225.00	1857-S	26,000	225.00
1845-O	47,500	225.00	1858	2,500	2,000.00
1846	20,100	225.00	1858-O	20,000	225.00
1846-O	81,800	225.00	1858-S	11,800	225.00
1847	862,300	225.00	1859	16,100	225.00
1847-O	571,500	225.00	1859-O	2,300	500.00
1848	145,500	225.00	1859-S	7,000	300.00
1848-O	35,800	225.00	1860	11,800	225.00
1849	653,600	225.00	1860-O	11,100	225.00
1849-O	23,900	225.00	1860-S	5,000	400.00
1850	291,500	225.00	1861	113,200	225.00
1850-O	57,500	225.00	1861-S	15,500	225.00
1851	176,300	225.00	1862	11,000	225.00
1851-O	263,000	225.00	1862-S	12,500	225.00
1852	263,100	225.00	1863	1,200	1,000.00
1852-O	18,000	225.00	1863-S	10,000	225.00
1853	201,300	225.00	1864	3,600	400.00
1853-O	51,000	225.00	1864-S	2,500	700.00
1854	54,200	225.00	1865	4,000	300.00
1854-O	52,500	225.00	1865-S	16,700	300.00
1854-S	123,800	225.00	1866-S	Part of 20,000	400.00
1855	121,700	225.00			

Type: Liberty head; with motto on Rev.

(The mint marks are on the Rev., under the eagle)

Date	Amount Minted	Value	Date	Amount Minted	Value
1866	3,800	225.00	1869	1,900	350.00
1866-S	Part of 20,000	225.00	1869-S	6,400	200.00
1867	3,100	225.00	1870	2,500	225.00
1867-S	9,000	225.00	1870-S	8,000	200.00
1868	10,700	200.00	1870-CC	5,900	450.00
1868-S	13,500	200.00	1871	1,800	225.00

Date	Amount Minted	Value	Date	Amount Minted	Value
1871-S	16,500	225.00	1886-S	826,000	200.00
1871-CC	7,200	350.00	1887	53,700	200.00
1872	1,600	400.00	1887-S	817,000	200.00
1872-S	17,300	225.00	1888	133,000	200.00
1872-CC	5,500	350.00	1888-O	21,300	200.00
1873	825	1000.00	1888-S	648,700	200.00
1873-S	12,000	225.00	1889	4,500	300.00
1873-CC	4,500	500.00	1889-S	425,400	200.00
1874	53,200	200.00	1890	58,000	200.00
1874-S	10,000	200.00	1890-CC	17,500	200.00
1874-CC	16,800	200.00	1891	91,900	200.00
1875	120	—	1891-CC	103,700	225.00
1875-CC	7,700	300.00	1892	797,600	200.00
1876	732	1000.00	1892-O	28,700	200.00
1876-S	5,000	300.00	1892-S	115,500	200.00
1876-CC	4,700	400.00	1892-CC	40,000	225.00
1877	817	1000.00	1893	1¾ million	200.00
1877-S	17,000	200.00	1893-O	17,000	200.00
1877-CC	3,300	500.00	1893-S	141,300	200.00
1878	73,800	200.00	1893-CC	14,000	200.00
1878-S	26,100	200.00	1894	2½ million	200.00
1878-CC	3,200	500.00	1894-O	107,500	200.00
1879	384,800	200.00	1894-S	25,000	200.00
1879-O	1,500	600.00	1895	567,800	200.00
1879-S	224,000	200.00	1895-O	98,000	200.00
1879-CC	1,800	1000.00	1895-S	49,000	200.00
1880	1⅔ million	200.00	1896	76,300	200.00
1880-O	9,200	200.00	1896-S	123,700	200.00
1880-S	506,200	200.00	1897	1 million	200.00
1880-CC	11,200	225.00	1897-O	42,500	200.00
1881	3¾ million	200.00	1897-S	234,700	200.00
1881-O	8,300	225.00	1898	812,200	200.00
1881-S	970,000	200.00	1898-S	473,600	200.00
1881-CC	24,000	200.00	1899	1¼ million	200.00
1882	2⅓ million	200.00	1899-O	37,000	200.00
1882-O	10,800	200.00	1899-S	841,000	200.00
1882-S	132,000	200.00	1900	294,000	200.00
1882-CC	6,800	225.00	1900-S	81,000	200.00
1883	208,700	200.00	1901	1¾ million	200.00
1883-O	800	1000.00	1901-O	72,000	200.00
1883-S	38,000	200.00	1901-S	2¾ million	200.00
1883-CC	12,000	225.00	1902	82,500	200.00
1884	76,900	200.00	1902-S	469,500	200.00
1884-S	124,200	200.00	1903	125,900	200.00
1884-CC	9,900	225.00	1903-O	112,800	200.00
1885	253,500	200.00	1903-S	538,000	200.00
1885-S	228,000	200.00	1904	162,000	200.00
1886	236,200	200.00	1904-O	108,900	200.00

Date	Amount Minted	Value	Date	Amount Minted	Value
1905	201,000	200.00	1906-D	981,000	200.00
1905-S	369,200	200.00	1907	1¼ million	200.00
1906	165,500	200.00	1907-S	210,500	200.00
1906-O	86,900	200.00	1907-D	1 million	200.00
1906-S	457,000	200.00			

Type: Indian head; without motto on Rev.

(The Mint marks are on the Rev., to the left of the value. The "1907 Periods" indicates a period at each end of "U.S.A." on the Rev.)

Date	Amount Minted	Value	Date	Amount Minted	Value
1907	239,400	350.00	1908	33,500	375.00
1907 Periods	542	2,000.00	1908-D	210,000	350.00

Type: Indian head; with motto on Rev.

Date	Amount Minted	Value	Date	Amount Minted	Value
1908	341,500	325.00	1913	442,100	325.00
1908-D	836,500	325.00	1913-S	66,000	325.00
1908-S	59,900	500.00	1914	151,000	325.00
1909	184,900	325.00	1914-D	343,500	325.00
1909-D	121,500	325.00	1914-S	208,000	325.00
1909-S	292,300	325.00	1915	351,100	325.00
1910	318,700	325.00	1915-S	59,000	400.00
1910-D	2⅓ million	325.00	1916-S	138,500	350.00
1910-S	811,000	325.00	1920-S	126,500	4500.00
1911	505,600	325.00	1926	1 million	325.00
1911-D	30,100	400.00	1930-S	96,000	2500.00
1911-S	51,000	350.00	1932	4½ million	325.00
1912	405,000	325.00	1933	312,500	———
1912-S	300,000	325.00			

20 DOLLAR GOLD PIECES (DOUBLE EAGLES)

Type: Liberty head; without motto on Rev.

(The mint marks are on the Rev., under the eagle)

Date	Amount Minted	Value	Date	Amount Minted	Value
1850	1¼ million	525.00	1858-O	35,200	550.00
1850-O	141,000	525.00	1858-S	846,700	500.00
1851	2 million	500.00	1859	43,600	525.00
1851-O	315,000	525.00	1859-O	9,100	1000.00
1852	2 million	500.00	1859-S	636,400	500.00
1852-O	190,000	525.00	1860	577,700	500.00
1853	1¼ million	500.00	1860-O	6,600	1200.00
1853-O	71,000	550.00	1860-S	544,900	500.00
1854	757,900	500.00	1861	3 million	500.00
1854-O	3,200	——	1861-O	5,000	800.00
1854-S	141,500	500.00	1861-S	768,000	500.00
1855	364,700	500.00	1862	92,100	500.00
1855-O	8,000	900.00	1862-S	854,200	500.00
1855-S	879,700	500.00	1863	142,800	500.00
1856	329,900	500.00	1863-S	966,600	500.00
1856-O	2,200	——	1864	204,300	500.00
1856-S	1¼ million	500.00	1864-S	793,700	500.00
1857	439,400	500.00	1865	351,200	500.00
1857-O	30,000	500.00	1865-S	1 million	500.00
1857-S	970,500	500.00	1866-S	Part of 842,200	525.00
1858	211,700	500.00			

Type: Liberty head; with motto on Rev. and "Twenty D."

(The mint marks are on the Rev., under the eagle)

Date	Amount Minted	Value	Date	Amount Minted	Value
1866	698,800	475.00	1872-S	780,000	475.00
1866-S	Part of 842,200	475.00	1872-CC	29,600	550.00
1867	251,065	475.00	1873	1¾ million	475.00
1867-S	920,700	475.00	1873-S	1 million	475.00
1868	98,600	475.00	1873-CC	22,400	550.00
1868-S	837,500	475.00	1874	366,800	475.00
1869	171,200	475.00	1874-S	1¼ million	475.00
1869-S	686,700	475.00	1874-CC	115,100	475.00
1870	155,200	475.00	1875	295,700	475.00
1870-S	982,000	475.00	1875-S	1¼ million	475.00
1870-CC	3,800	——	1875-CC	111,100	475.00
1871	80,100	475.00	1876	583,900	475.00
1871-S	928,000	475.00	1876-S	1½ million	475.00
1871-CC	14,700	800.00	1876-CC	138,400	525.00
1872	251,900	475.00			

Type: Liberty head; with motto on Rev. and "Twenty Dollars."

(The mint marks are on the Rev., under the eagle)

1877	397,700	475.00	1878-CC	13,200	535.00
1877-S	1¾ million	475.00	1879	207,600	475.00
1877-CC	42,600	525.00	1879-O	2,300	1500.00
1878	543,600	475.00	1879-S	1¼ million	475.00
1878-S	1¾ million	475.00	1879-CC	10,700	550.00

Date	Amount Minted	Value	Date	Amount Minted	Value
1880	51,500	475.00	1893	344,300	475.00
1880-S	836,000	475.00	1893-S	996,200	475.00
1881	2,300	1650.00	1893-CC	18,400	525.00
1881-S	727,000	475.00	1894	1⅓ million	475.00
1882	630	3000.00	1894-S	1 million	475.00
1882-S	1¼ million	475.00	1895	1 million	475.00
1882-CC	39,100	500.00	1895-S	1¼ million	475.00
1883	About 100 proofs	——	1896	792,700	475.00
1883-S	1¼ million	475.00	1896-S	1½ million	475.00
1883-CC	60,000	500.00	1897	1⅓ million	475.00
1884	71 proofs	——	1897-S	1½ million	475.00
1884-S	916,000	475.00	1898	170,500	475.00
1884-CC	81,100	500.00	1898-S	2½ million	475.00
1885	828	2000.00	1899	1⅔ million	475.00
1885-S	683,500	475.00	1899-S	2 million	475.00
1885-CC	9,500	550.00	1900	1¾ million	475.00
1886	1,100	2000.00	1900-S	2½ million	475.00
1887	121 proofs	——	1901	111,500	475.00
1887-S	283,000	475.00	1901-S	1½ million	475.00
1888	226,300	475.00	1902	31,300	475.00
1888-S	859,600	475.00	1902-S	1¾ million	475.00
1889	44,100	475.00	1903	287,400	475.00
1889-S	774,700	475.00	1903-S	954,000	475.00
1889-CC	30,900	475.00	1904	6¼ million	475.00
1890	76,000	475.00	1904-S	5¼ million	475.00
1890-S	802,700	475.00	1905	59,000	475.00
1890-CC	91,200	475.00	1905-S	1¾ million	475.00
1891	1,400	1000.00	1906	69,700	475.00
1891-S	1¼ million	475.00	1906-S	2 million	475.00
1891-CC	5,000	1000.00	1906-D	620,200	475.00
1892	4,500	700.00	1907	1½ million	475.00
1892-S	930,100	475.00	1907-S	2¼ million	475.00
1892-CC	27,300	475.00	1907-D	842,200	475.00

**Type: Liberty standing (St. Gaudens design).
Date in Roman Numerals, MCMVII.**

1907   11,200   2,000.00

Type: Liberty standing; date in normal numerals; without motto on Rev.

(The mint mark is on the Obv., over the date)

Date	Amount Minted	Value	Date	Amount Minted	Value
1907	361,700	545.00	1908-D	663,700	545.00
1908	4¼ million	545.00			

Type: Liberty standing; with motto on Rev.

(The mint marks are on the Obv., over the date)

Date	Amount Minted	Value	Date	Amount Minted	Value
1908	156,400	545.00	1914	95,300	545.00
1908-D	349,500	545.00	1914-D	453,000	545.00
1908-S	22,000	650.00	1914-S	1½ million	545.00
1909	Part of 161,300	545.00	1915	152,000	545.00
1909 over 8	Part of 161,300	545.00	1915-S	567,500	545.00
1909-D	52,500	545.00	1916-S	796,000	545.00
1909-S	2¾ million	545.00	1920	228,200	545.00
1910	482,200	545.00	1920-S	558,000	4500.00
1910-D	429,000	545.00	1921	528,500	6500.00
1910-S	2¼ million	545.00	1922	1⅓ million	545.00
1911	197,300	545.00	1922-S	2⅔ million	545.00
1911-D	846,500	545.00	1923	566,000	545.00
1911-S	775,700	545.00	1923-D	1⅔ million	545.00
1912	149,800	545.00	1924	4⅓ million	545.00
1913	168,800	545.00	1924-D	3 million	545.00
1913-D	393,500	545.00	1924-S	3 million	545.00
1913-S	34,000	545.00	1925	2¾ million	545.00

Date	Amount Minted	Value	Date	Amount Minted	Value
1925-D	3 million	650.00	1928	8¾ million	545.00
1925-S	3¾ million	545.00	1929	1¾ million	2,000.00
1926	816,700	545.00	1930-S	74,000	5,000.00
1926-D	481,000	650.00	1931	3 million	3,500.00
1926-S	2 million	545.00	1931-D	106,500	3,500.00
1927	3 million	545.00	1932	1 million	4,000.00
1927-D	180,000	——	1933	445,500	not issued
1927-S	3 million	2000.00			

Pioneer Gold Coins

Coinage of the Territorial and Private Mints

(The valuations are for coins in VG to F condition)
(Beware of Copies)

BALDWIN & CO.

San Francisco, California

Horseman with lariat. Rev. Eagle.

10 Dollars 1850 .... 4,000.00

"Baldwin & Co" on head band of Liberty. Rev. Eagle.

5 Dollars 1850 .... 600.00
10 Dollars 1851 .... 2,000.00
20 Dollars 1851 .... ——

AUGUST BECHTLER

Rutherford, North Carolina

Value and legend. Rev. Weight and legend. The coins are
undated but were struck from 1842 to 1852.

1 Dollar ND. One variety 200.00
5 Dollars ND. Three varieties 450.00

CHRISTOPHER BECHTLER

Rutherford, North Carolina

Value and legend. Rev. Weight and legend. The coins are
undated, but were struck from 1831 to 1842.

1   Dollar ND. Four varieties 225.00
2½ Dollars ND. Seven varieties 450.00
5   Dollars ND. Six varieties... 500.00
5   Dollars August 1, 1834. Two varieties...................................... 525.00

The valuations listed in this book closely approximate how much established coin dealers will pay for any material needed in their stock.

EPHRAIM BRASHER

New York

Radiant sun over mountains. Rev. Eagle with "EB" punched on
either the wing or breast. The famous Brasher Doubloon.

Doubloon 1787   Extremely Rare.. ——
½ Doubloon 1787 Extremely Rare.. ——

CINCINNATI MINING & TRADING CO.

San Francisco, California

Indian Head. Rev. Eagle

5 Dollars 1849 .... ——
10 Dollars 1849 .... ——

CLARK, GRUBER & CO.

Denver, Colorado

View of Pikes Peak. Rev. Eagle.

10 Dollars 1860 ....   600.00
20 Dollars 1860 .... 5,000.00

"Clark & Co." on head band of Liberty. Rev. Eagle.

2½	Dollars 1860	200.00
5	Dollars 1860	300.00

"Pikes Peak" on head band of Liberty. Rev. Eagle.

2½	Dollars 1861	200.00
5	Dollars 1861	300.00
10	Dollars 1861	350.00
20	Dollars 1861	1,250.00

J. J. CONWAY & CO.

Georgia Gulch, Colorado

Name of company. Rev. Value and "Pikes Peak."
Undated but struck in 1861.

2½	Dollars ND	—
5	Dollars ND	—
10	Dollars ND	—

DUBOSQ & CO.

San Francisco, California

"Dubosq & Co." on head band of Liberty. Rev. Eagle.

5 Dollars 1850 .... ——
10 Dollars 1850 .... ——

DUNBAR & CO.

San Francisco, California

"Dunbar & Co." on head band of Liberty. Rev. Eagle.

5 Dollars 1851 .... ——

AUGUSTUS HUMBERT

U.S. Assayer of gold, San Francisco, California

Eagle. Rev. Four line legend in tablet.

10 Dollars 1852 ....   400.00
20 Dollars 1852 ....   1,250.00

Eagle. Rev. Small 50, star or circle in center of otherwise blank
Rev. Octagonal shaped with lettered edge.

50 Dollars 1851. Five varieties **2,000.00**

Eagle. Rev. Machine made criss-cross of circular lines. Octagonal
shaped with reeded edge.

50 Dollars 1851, 52. Three varieties **2,000.00**

KELLOGG & CO.

San Francisco, California

"Kellogg & Co." on head band of Liberty. Rev. Standard Eagle.
20 Dollars 1854, 55 .... 700.00

Obv. Similar to above. Rev. Eagle holding shield.
50 Dollars 1855 .... ——

MASSACHUSETTS & CALIFORNIA CO.

San Francisco, California

Arms supported by bear and stag. Rev. Value in wreath.
5 Dollars 1849. Four varieties.. ——

MINERS BANK

San Francisco, California

Name and value. Rev. Eagle.

10 Dollars 1849 .... **2,000.00**

MOFFAT & CO.

San Francisco, California

"Moffat & Co." on head band of Liberty. Rev. Eagle.

5 Dollars 1849, 50	**300.00**
10 Dollars 1849, 52	**475.00**
20 Dollars 1853	**700.00**

THE MORMONS

Salt Lake City, Utah

Eye and Bishop's Mitre. Rev. Clasped hands.

2½	Dollars 1849	**850.00**
5	Dollars 1849, 50	**800.00**
10	Dollars 1849	——
20	Dollars 1849	——

Lion. Rev. Beehive on breast of eagle.

5 Dollars 1860 .... 1,000.00

NORRIS, GRIEG & NORRIS
San Francisco, California

Eagle. Rev. Legend.

5 Dollars 1849. Plain or reeded edge............................... 650.00

OREGON EXCHANGE CO.
Oregon City, Oregon

Beaver and initials. Rev. Legend.

5 Dollars 1849 .... 1,750.00
10 Dollars 1849 .... 6,000.00

J. S. ORMSBY

San Francisco, California

"J.S.O." Rev. Value. Undated but struck in 1849.

5 Dollars ND .... ——
10 Dollars ND .... ——

PACIFIC CO.

San Francisco, California

Liberty Cap. Rev. Eagle.

5 Dollars 1849 .... ——
10 Dollars 1849 .... ——

JOHN PARSONS & CO.

Tarryall Mines, Colorado

*Stamping machine. Rev. Eagle and "Pikes Peak Gold." Undated
but struck in 1861.*

2½ Dollars ND .... ——
5 Dollars ND .... ——

SHULTS & CO.

San Francisco, California

"Shults & Co." on head band of Liberty. Rev. Eagle.

5 Dollars 1851 .... **4,000.00**

TEMPLETON REID

Lumpkin County, Georgia

Legend on each side.

2½ Dollars 1830 .... ——
5   Dollars 1830 .... ——
10   Dollars 1830 .... ——
10   Dollars ND .... ——

TEMPLETON REID

San Francisco, California

Legend on each side.

10 Dollars 1849 .... ——
25 Dollars 1849 .... ——

UNITED STATES ASSAY OFFICE OF GOLD

San Francisco, California

Eagle. Rev. Legend in tablet.

10 Dollars 1852, 53. Two varieties 500.00
20 Dollars 1853. Two varieties 700.00

Eagle. Rev. Machine made criss-cross of circular lines. Octagonal shaped.

50 Dollars 1852. Two varieties 1,500.00

WASS, MOLITOR & CO.

San Francisco, California

"W.M. & Co." on head band of Liberty. Rev. Eagle.

5 Dollars 1852 .... 600.00
10 Dollars 1852, 55. Two varieties 450.00
20 Dollars 1855. Two varieties 1,750.00

Liberty head. Rev. Name and value.

50 Dollars 1855 .... **3,000.00**

United States Proof Sets

A Proof Set contains five coins; the 1c, 5c, 10c, 25c and 50c pieces. From 1936 through 1942, unequal amounts were struck of each denomination; from 1950 to date equal amounts have been struck. In the column under Amount Minted, the figure shows the total number of *complete* sets minted in each year. In 1942, two types of proof 5 Cent pieces were struck, the standard coin and the one with silver content; hence, there are two listings for the 1942 Proof Set. In 1973 and 1974, the dollar was added to the set. In 1975, the Proof Set contained the 1975-S 1c, 5c and 10c pieces plus the 1976-S Bicentennial 25c, 50c and dollar. Because of speculation, the valuations are subject to fluctuation.

Year	Amount Minted	Value	Year	Amount Minted	Value	Year	Amount Minted	Value
1936	3,837	3,000.00	1959	1,149,291	13.50	1970 small date	2,632,810	80.0
1937	5,542	2,000.00	1960 small date	1,691,600	24.50			
1938	8,045	1,000.00	1960 large date		12.50	1970 large date		8.0
1939	8,795	850.00	1961	3,028,244	11.50	1971	3,224,138	3.5
1940	11,246	700.00	1962	3,218,039	11.50	1972	3,267,667	3.5
1941	15,287	625.00	1963	3,075,645	11.50	1973	2,769,624	5.7
1942 with one nickel	21,120	625.00	1964	3,949,634	11.50	1974	2,617,350	6.0
1942 with two nickels		825.00	1965 special mint set	2,360,000	3.00	1975	2,845,451	8.5
1950	51,386	375.00	1966 special mint set	2,261,583	5.50	1976		
1951	57,500	225.00	1967 special mint set	1,863,344	8.00	3-pc. set	3,295,715	9.5
1952	81,980	130.00	1968 proof set	3,041,509	3.75	1976	4,149,730	5.0
1953	128,800	85.00	1969	2,934,631	3.75	1977	3,251,152	4.5
1954	233,300	47.50				1978	3,127,781	6.7
1955	378,200	42.50				1979 Type I	3,677,175	12.0
1956	669,384	21.00				1979 Type II		100.0
1957	1,247,952	13.00				1980	3,547,030	5.7
1958	875,652	16.50				1981 Type I	4,063,083	6.7
						1981 Type II		135.0
						1982		12.0

United States Paper Money

Large Size Notes, Small Size Notes, Fractional Currency

1 DOLLAR NOTES

Torn, frayed or excessively worn notes command little or no premium.

Type of Issue	Series	Portrait or Main Design	Value
LARGE SIZE NOTES			**USED CONDITION**
U.S. Note (Legal Tender)	1862	Chase	20.00
"	1869	Washington	25.00
"	1874	Washington	15.00
"	1875	Washington	9.00
"	1878	Washington	9.00
"	1880	Washington	10.00
"	1917	Washington	4.00
"	1923	Washington (Red Seal)	6.50
Silver Certificate	1886	Martha Washington	16.00
"	1891	Martha Washington	10.00
"	1896	George and Martha Washington (on Rev.)	25.00
"	1899	Lincoln and Grant	4.00
"	1923	Washington (Blue Seal)	3.00
Treasury or Coin Note	1890	Stanton	25.00
"	1891	Stanton	10.00
National Bank Note	Old (original)	Two maidens standing	20.00
"	1875	Two maidens standing	20.00
Federal Reserve Bank Note	1918	Washington	4.00
SMALL SIZE NOTES			**NEW CONDITION**
U.S. Note (Red Seal)	1928	Washington	25.00
Silver Certificate (Blue Seal)	1928 (A-E)	Washington	4.00
"	1934	Washington	2.50
Silver Certificate (Blue Seal)	1935 (A-H*)	Washington	1.25
"	1957 (A-B)	Washington	1.25
Hawaiian Issue (Brown Seal)	1935-A	Washington	12.00
Armed Forces Issue (Yellow Seal)	1935-A	Washington	10.00
Federal Reserve (Green Seal)	1963 (A-B)	Washington	1.00
"	1969 (A-D)	Washington	1.00
"	1974	Washington	Current

* 1935-G with and without motto

2 DOLLAR NOTES

Torn, frayed or excessively worn notes command little or no premium.

			USED CONDITION
LARGE SIZE NOTES			
U.S. Note (Legal Tender)	1862	Hamilton	20.00
"	1869	Jefferson	22.50
"	1874	Jefferson	20.00
"	1875	Jefferson	12.00
"	1878	Jefferson	12.00
"	1880	Jefferson	7.50
"	1917	Jefferson	6.00

Type of Issue	Series	Portrait or Main Design	Value
LARGE SIZE NOTES		**USED CONDITION**	
Silver Certificate	1886	Gen. Hancock	24.00
"	1891	William Windom	22.50
"	1896	Fulton and Morse (on Rev.)	32.00
"	1899	Washington	12.00
Treasury or Coin Note	1890	Gen. McPherson	50.00
"	1891	Gen McPherson	20.00
National Bank Note	Old (original)	Large, horizontal "lazy" 2	80.00
"	1875	Large, horizontal "lazy" 2	80.00
Federal Reserve Bank Note	1918	Jefferson	15.00
SMALL SIZE NOTES		**NEW CONDITION**	
U.S. Note	1928 (A-G)	Jefferson	5.00
"	1953 (A-C)	Jefferson	2.50
"	1963 (A)	Jefferson	2.50

5 DOLLAR NOTES

Torn, frayed or excessively worn notes command little or no premium.

Type of Issue	Series	Portrait or Main Design	Value
LARGE SIZE NOTES		**USED CONDITION**	
Demand Note	1861	Hamilton	150.00
U.S. Note (Legal Tender)	1862	Hamilton	17.00
"	1863	Hamilton	17.00
"	1869	Jackson	22.00
"	1875	Jackson	12.00
"	1878	Jackson	12.00
"	1880	Jackson	10.00
"	1907	Jackson	10.00
Silver Certificate	1886	Grant	70.00
"	1891	Grant	25.00
"	1896	Grant and Sheridan (on Rev.)	65.00
"	1899	Indian Chief, Onepapa	40.00
"	1923	Lincoln	25.00
Treasury or Coin Note	1890	Gen. Thomas	32.00
"	1891	Gen. Thomas	25.00
National Bank Note	Old (original)	Landing of Columbus (on Rev.)	20.00
"	1875	Landing of Columbus (on Rev.)	20.00
"	1882	Garfield; brown back	15.00
"	1882	Garfield; "1882-1908" on back	15.00
"	1882	Garfield; "Five Dollars" on back	18.00
"	1902	Harrison; red seal	11.00
"	1902	Harrison; blue seal; "1902-1908" on back	7.00
"	1902	Harrison; blue seal only	7.00
Federal Reserve Bank Note	1915	Lincoln	9.00
"	1918	Lincoln	9.00
Federal Reserve Note	1914	Lincoln; red seal	7.00
"	1914	Lincoln; blue seal	6.00
National Gold Bank Note	1870-74	Gold coins on back	200.00

Type of Issue	Series	Portrait or Main Design	Value
SMALL SIZE NOTES			**NEW CONDITION**
U.S. Note	1928 (A-F)	Lincoln	6.50
"	1953 (A-C)	Lincoln	5.50
"	1963	Lincoln	5.10
Silver Certificate	1934 (A-D)	Lincoln	6.00
"	1953 (A-B)	Lincoln	5.25
National Bank Note	1929	Lincoln	15.00
Federal Reserve Bank Note	1929	Lincoln	10.00
Federal Reserve Note	1928 (A-D)	Lincoln	5.50
"	1934 (A-D)	Lincoln	5.25
"	1950 (A-E)	Lincoln	5.00
"	1963 (A)	Lincoln	5.00
"	1969 (A-C)	Lincoln	5.00
"	1974	Lincoln	Current
Hawaiian Issue (Brown Seal)	1934 (A)	Lincoln	25.00
Armed Forces Issue (Yellow Seal)	1934-A	Lincoln	20.00

10 DOLLAR NOTES

Torn, frayed or excessively worn notes command little or no premium.

LARGE SIZE NOTES			**USED CONDITION**
Demand Note	1861	Lincoln	275.00
U.S. Note (Legal Tender)	1862	Lincoln	40.00
"	1863	Lincoln	40.00
"	1869	Webster	45.00
"	1875	Webster	22.00
U.S. Note (Legal Tender)	1878	Webster	22.00
"	1880	Webster	17.00
"	1901	Lewis and Clark; bison	40.00
"	1923	Jackson	70.00
Compound Interest Note	1863-65	Chase	175.00
Interest Bearing Note (one year)	1864	Chase	375.00
Refunding Certificate	1879	Franklin	140.00
Silver Certificate	1878	Robert Morris	500.00
"	1880	Robert Morris	70.00
"	1886	Thomas Hendricks	50.00
"	1891	Thomas Hendricks	22.00
"	1908	Thomas Hendricks	20.00
Treasury or Coin Note	1890	Gen. Sheridan	50.00
"	1891	Gen. Sheridan	25.00
National Bank Note	Old (original)	De Soto at the Mississippi (on Rev.)	40.00
"	1875	De Soto at the Mississippi (on Rev.)	40.00
"	1882	Franklin with kite; brown back	25.00
"	1882	Same with "1882-1908" on back	25.00
"	1882	Same with "Ten Dollars" on back	28.00
"	1902	McKinley; red seal	20.00
"	1902	McKinley; blue seal; "1902-1908" on back	12.00
"	1902	McKinley; blue seal only	12.00

Type of Issue	Series	Portrait or Main Design	Value
LARGE SIZE NOTES			**USED CONDITION**
Federal Reserve Bank Note	1915	Jackson	22.50
''	1918	Jackson	22.50
Federal Reserve Note	1914	Jackson; red seal	13.00
''	1914	Jackson; blue seal	11.00
National Gold Bank Note	1870-75	Gold coins on back	250.00
Gold Certificate	1907	Michael Hillegas	13.00
''	1922	Michael Hillegas	13.00
SMALL SIZE NOTES			**NEW CONDITION**
Silver Certificate	1933	Hamilton	1,200.00
''	1934 (A-D)	Hamilton	12.00
''	1953 (A-B)	Hamilton	11.00
National Bank Note	1929	Hamilton	20.00
Federal Reserve Bank Note	1929	Hamilton	12.00
Federal Reserve Note	1928 (A-C)	Hamilton	10.50
''	1934 (A-D)	Hamilton	10.00
''	1950 (A-E)	Hamilton	10.00
''	1963 (A)	Hamilton	10.00
''	1969 (A-C)	Hamilton	10.00
''	1974	Hamilton	Current
Hawaiian Issue (Brown Seal)	1934-A	Hamilton	35.00
Armed Forces Issue (Yellow Seal)	1934 (A)	Hamilton	30.00
Gold Certificate	1928	Hamilton	45.00

20 DOLLAR NOTES

Torn, frayed or excessively worn notes command little or no premium.

	Series	Portrait or Main Design	Value
LARGE SIZE NOTES			**USED CONDITION**
Demand Note	1861	Liberty Standing	1,200.00
U.S. Note (Legal Tender)	1862	Liberty Standing	45.00
''	1863	Liberty Standing	45.00
''	1869	Hamilton	100.00
''	1875	Hamilton	30.00
''	1878	Hamilton	25.00
''	1880	Hamilton	22.50
Compound Interest Note	1863-65	Lincoln	400.00
Interest Bearing Note (one year)	1864	Lincoln	750.00
Silver Certificate	1878	Stephen Decatur	600.00
''	1880	Stephen Decatur	125.00
''	1886	Daniel Manning	100.00
''	1891	Daniel Manning	30.00
Treasury or Coin Note	1890	John Marshall	100.00
''	1891	John Marshall	120.00
National Bank Note	Old (original)	Baptism of Pocahontas (on Rev.)	60.00
''	1875	Baptism of Pocahontas (on Rev.)	60.00
''	1882	Battle of Lexington; brown back	28.00
''	1882	Same with "1882-1908" on back	28.00
''	1882	Same with "Twenty Dollars" on back	32.00
''	1902	Hugh McCulloch; red seal	25.00
''	1902	Hugh McCulloch; blue seal; "1902-1908" on back	22.00

Type of Issue	Series	Portrait or Main Design	Value
LARGE SIZE NOTES			**USED CONDITION**
National Bank Note	1902	Hugh McCulloch; blue seal only	22.00
Federal Reserve Bank Note	1915	Cleveland	40.00
"	1918	Cleveland	40.00
Federal Reserve Note	1914	Cleveland; red seal	25.00
"	1914	Cleveland; blue seal	22.00
National Gold Bank Note	1870-75	Gold coins on back	376.00
Gold Certificate	1863	Eagle on shield	——
"	1882	Garfield	32.00
"	1905	Washington	90.00
"	1906	Washington	27.00
"	1922	Washington	27.00
SMALL SIZE NOTES			**NEW CONDITION**
National Bank Note	1929	Jackson	30.00
Federal Reserve Bank Note	1929	Jackson	22.00
Federal Reserve Note	1928 (A-C)	Jackson	21.00
"	1934 (A-D)	Jackson	20.00
"	1950 (A-E)	Jackson	20.00
"	1963 (A)	Jackson	20.00
"	1969 (A-C)	Jackson	20.00
"	1974	Jackson	Current
Hawaiian Issue (Brown Seal)	1934 (A)	Jackson	50.00
Gold Certificate	1928	Jackson	50.00

50 DOLLAR NOTES

Torn, frayed or excessively worn notes command little or no premium.

LARGE SIZE NOTES			**USED CONDITION**
U.S. Note (Legal Tender)	1862	Hamilton	375.00
"	1863	Hamilton	325.00
"	1869	Henry Clay	700.00
"	1874	Franklin	165.00
"	1875	Franklin	150.00
"	1878	Franklin	150.00
"	1880	Franklin	70.00
Compound Interest Note	1863-65	Hamilton	Rare
Interest Bearing Note (one year)	1864	Hamilton	Rare
Interest Bearing Note (two years)	1863	Three females	Rare
Interest Bearing Note (three years)	1861	Large eagle	Rare
"	1864	Large eagle	Rare
"	1865	Large eagle	Rare
Silver Certificate	1878	Edward Everett	650.00
"	1880	Edward Everett	500.00
"	1891	Edward Everett	85.00
Treasury or Coin Note	1891	William Seward	1,200.00
National Bank Note	Old (original)	Embarkation of the Pilgrims (on Rev.)	450.00
"	1875	Embarkation of the Pilgrims (on Rev.)	450.00
"	1882	Washington Crossing the Delaware and at prayer; brown back	75.00
"	1882	Same with "1882-1908" on back	75.00

Type of Issue	Series	Portrait or Main Design	Value
SMALL SIZE NOTES			**USED CONDITION**
Federal Reserve Bank Note	1929	Grant	**51.00**
Federal Reserve Note	1928 (A)	Grant	**50.00**
"	1934 (A-D)	Grant	**50.00**
"	1950 (A-E)	Grant	**50.00**
"	1963-A	Grant	**50.00**
"	1969 (A-C)	Grant	**50.00**
"	1974	Grant	**Current**
Gold Certificate	1928	Grant	**150.00**

100 DOLLAR NOTES

Torn, frayed or excessively worn notes command little or no premium.

LARGE SIZE NOTES			**USED CONDITION**
U.S. Note (Legal Tender)	1862	Large eagle	**600.00**
"	1863	Large eagle	**600.00**
"	1869	Lincoln	**1,000.00**
"	1875	Lincoln	**500.00**
"	1878	Lincoln	**500.00**
"	1880	Lincoln	**150.00**
Compound Interest Note	1863-65	Washington standing	**700.00**
Interest Bearing Note (one year)	1864	Washington standing	**Rare**
Interest Bearing Note (two years)	1863	Agriculture and Industry	**Rare**
Interest Bearing Note (three years)	1861	Gen. Scott	**Rare**
"	1865	Gen. Scott	**Rare**
Silver Certificate	1878	Monroe	**500.00**
"	1880	Monroe	**400.00**
"	1891	Monroe	**150.00**
Treasury or Coin Note	1890	Commodore Farragut	**1,000.00**
"	1891	Commodore Farragut	**1,000.00**
National Bank Note	Old (original)	Signing the Declaration of Independence (on Rev.)	**400.00**
"	1875	Signing the Declaration of Independence (on Rev.)	**400.00**
"	1882	Commodore Perry leaving his flagship; brown back	**125.00**
"	1882	Same with "1882-1908" on back	**120.00**
"	1882	Same with "One Hundred Dollars" on back	**Rare**
"	1902	John Knox; red seal	**110.00**
"	1902	John Knox; blue seal; "1902 1908" on back	**100.00**
"	1902	John Knox; blue seal only	**100.00**
Federal Reserve Note	1914	Franklin; red seal	**100.00**
"	1914	Franklin; blue seal	**100.00**
National Gold Bank Note	1870-75	Gold coins on back	**1,400.00**
Gold Certificate	1863	Eagle on shield	——
"	1870-71	Thomas Benton	——
"	1875	Thomas Benton	——
"	1882	Thomas Benton	**110.00**
"	1922	Thomas Benton	**125.00**

Type of Issue	Series	Portrait or Main Design	Value
LARGE SIZE NOTES			**USED CONDITION**
National Bank Note	1882	Commodore Perry leaving his flagship; brown back	125.00
"	1882	Same with "1882-1908" on back	120.00
"	1882	Same with "One Hundred Dollars" on back	**Rare**
"	1902	John Knox; red seal	110.00
"	1902	John Knox; blue seal; "1902-1908" on back	100.00
"	1902	John Knox; blue seal only	100.00
Federal Reserve Note	1914	Franklin; red seal	100.00
"	1914	Franklin; blue seal	100.00
National Gold Bank Note	1870-75	Gold coins on back	1,400.00
Gold Certificate	1863	Eagle on shield	——
"	1870-71	Thomas Benton	——
"	1875	Thomas Benton	——
"	1882	Thomas Benton	110.00
"	1922	Thomas Benton	125.00
SMALL SIZE NOTES			**NEW CONDITION**
National Bank Note	1929	Franklin	100.00
Federal Reserve Bank Note	1929	Franklin	100.00
Federal Reserve Note	1928 (A)	Franklin	100.00
"	1934 (A-D)	Franklin	100.00
"	1950 (A-E)	Franklin	100.00
"	1963-A	Franklin	100.00
"	1969 (A-C)	Franklin	100.00
"	1974	Franklin	**Current**
U.S. Note (Legal Tender)	1966 (A)	Franklin	100.00
Gold Certificate	1928	Franklin	150.00

Fractional Currency

Torn, frayed or excessively worn notes command little or no premium.

3 CENT NOTES

Years of Issue	Description	Used
1864-1869	Small head of Washington.	2.00

5 CENT NOTES

1862-1863	Facsimile of a 5 Cent postage stamp with head of Jefferson	2.00
1862-1863	Same as above but with perforated edges.	2.50
1863-1867	Head of Washington in bronze oval frame. Brown back.	2.00
1864-1869	Head of Spencer M. Clark. Green back.	2.00
1864-1869	Same as above but with red back.	3.00

10 CENT NOTES

Years of Issue	Description	Used
1862-1863	Facsimile of a 10 Cent postage stamp with head of Washington.	2.00
1862-1863	Same as above but with perforated edges.	2.50
1863-1867	Head of Washington in bronze oval frame. Green back.	2.00
1864-1869	Head of Washington. A bronze "10" in each corner. Green back.	2.50
1864-1869	Same as above but with red back.	3.00
1869-1875	Bust of Liberty.	1.25
1874-1876	Head of William M. Meredith. Green seal.	1.25
1874-1876	Same as above but with red seal.	1.00

15 CENT NOTES

1869-1875	Bust of Columbia.	3.50
Not Issued	Heads of Grant and Sherman. Separate front and back. Green back.	20.00
Not Issued	Same as above but with red back.	20.00

25 CENT NOTES

1862-1863	Facsimiles of five 5 Cent postage stamps with head of Jefferson.	3.00
1862-1863	Same as above but with perforated edges.	4.00
1863-1867	Head of Washington in bronze oval frame. Purple back.	1.75
1864-1869	Bust of Fessenden. Green back.	1.75
1864-1869	Same as above but with red back.	3.00
1869-1875	Bust of Washington.	1.25
1874-1876	Bust of Robert V. Walker.	.75

50 CENT NOTES

1862-1863	Facsimiles of five 10 Cent postage stamps with head of Washington.	3.00
1862-1863	Same as above but with perforated edges.	5.00
1863-1867	Head of Washington in bronze oval frame. Red back.	1.75
1864-1869	Bust of Gen. Spinner. Green back with a "50" at each end.	1.75
1864-1869	Same as above but with red back.	2.00
1864-1869	Bust of Gen. Spinner. Green back with "50" in center.	1.75
1864-1869	Seated figure of Justice. Green back.	2.00
1864-1869	Same as above but with red back.	2.00
1869-1875	Bust of Lincoln.	4.00
1869-1875	Bust of E. M. Stanton.	2.00
1869-1875	Bust of Samuel Dexter.	2.50
1874-1876	Bust of William Crawford.	1.50

Confederate States of America

Torn, frayed or excessively worn notes command little or no premium.

PAPER MONEY ISSUES

All notes were issued from Richmond, Virginia, except the few 1861 issues listed as from Montgomery, Alabama.

In recent years, facsimiles have been made of many Confederate notes. Many people mistake them for genuine pieces. They are usually on much heavier paper and are invariably in new condition. In many cases, the word, "Facsimile" may actually be found in quite small letters somewhere on the note.

Confederate notes will sometimes be found cut or slit in a regular pattern, or with holes punched through. These indicate concellation by the Confederacy, and are worth less than uncancelled specimens.

For further general comment on Confederate currency, please see under "United States Paper Money" in the General Information following the Preface.

50 CENT NOTES

Year	Portrait or Main Design	Used
1863	Jefferson Davis. Blank Rev.	.75
1864	Similar to above except for date.	.60

1 DOLLAR NOTES

1862	Steamship with sails; female standing at left; Lucy Pickens at right. Blank Rev.	3.00
1862	Similar to above, but overprinted with a large green "1" and "ONE." Blank Rev.	5.00
1862	C. Clay. Blank Rev.	4.00
1863	Similar to above except for date.	3.25
1864	Similar to above except for date.	1.00

2 DOLLAR NOTES

1861	The "South" attacking the "North" with sword; J. P. Benjamin at left. Blank Rev.	25.00
1862	The "South" attacking the "North" with sword; J. P. Benjamin at left. Blank Rev.	3.25
1862	Similar to above but overprinted with a large green "2" and "TWO." Blank Rev.	14.50
1862	Ornamented "2" in center; J. P. Benjamin at right. Blank Rev.	2.50
1863	Similar to above except for date.	2.50
1864	Similar to above except for date.	2.00

5 DOLLAR NOTES

1861	Liberty seated with shield and eagle, a "5" in front; sailor at left. Blank Rev.	200.00
1861	"V" in upper left; "5" in upper right. Blue Rev.	200.00
1861	Five females seated; standing female at left; Washington at right. Blank Rev.	22.50
1861	Child at left; blacksmith at right. Blank Rev.	27.50
1861	C. Memminger; Minerva at right, "V" below. Blank rev.	13.00
1861	Similar to above except that "FIVE" is below Minerva. Blank Rev.	5.00

Year	Portrait or Main Design	Used
1861	Negroes loading cotton on ship at left; Indian girl at right. Blank Rev.	225.00
1861	Female seated on cotton bale; sailor at left. Blank Rev.	3.00
1861	Sailor and cotton bales; C. Memminger at left; two females at right. Blank Rev.	3.00
1862	State Capitol at Richmond, Va.; C. Memminger at right. Blue Rev.	2.00
1863	Similar to above except for date.	2.00
1864	Similar to above except for date.	1.50

10 DOLLAR NOTES

1861	Liberty seated with shield and eagle; female at left. Blank Rev.	3.00
1861	Indian family; female with trident at left; female with "X" at right. Blank Rev.	30.00
1861	Cotton wagon; male bust at left; harvester at right. Blank Rev.	35.00
1861	R. Hunter at left; a child at right. Blank Rev.	12.00
1861	Female with anchor; R. Hunter at left; C. Memminger at right. Blank Rev.	5.00
1861	Similar to above except that an "X" is overprinted in red at each side of the female. Blank Rev.	5.00
1861	Liberty with eagle and shield at upper left; small train at right. Blank Rev.	250.00
1861	Two females with urn at upper left; small train at right. Blank Rev.	2.00
1861	Negro with cotton; landscape at right. Blank Rev.	6.00
1861	Military figures at dinner; R. Hunter at left; Minerva at right. Blank Rev.	3.00
1862	Female leaning on cotton bales, ships in rear; R. Hunter at right. Blank Rev.	3.00
1862	Female seated with wheat; R. Hunter at right. Blank Rev.	600.00
1862	State Capitol at Columbia, S. C.; R. Hunter at right. Blue Rev.	1.50
1863	Similar to above except for date.	1.50
1864	Horses pulling artillery pieces; R. Hunter at right. Blue Rev.	1.50

20 DOLLAR NOTES

1861	Full masted sailing ship. Blank Rev.	2.50
1861	Three females in center, Liberty standing at left. Blank Rev.	60.00
1861	Full masted sailing ship; sailor at left. Blank Rev.	2.00
1861	Female with globe; female at left; blacksmith at right. Blank Rev.	200.00
1861	Female between Cupid and beehive; Vice President Stephens at left; female with anchor at right. Blank Rev.	1.75
1861	Vice President Stephens. Blank Rev.	17.50
1862	Liberty seated with shield of the Confederacy; R. Hunter at right. Blank Rev.	400.00
1862	State Capitol at Nashville, Tenn.; Stephens at right. Blue Rev.	4.00
1863	Similar to above except for date.	1.50
1864	Similar to above except for date.	1.25

50 DOLLAR NOTES

1861	Three Negro farm workers. Blank Rev. Montgomery, Ala.	500.00
1861	Two females on cotton bale; Justice at left; Washington at right. Blank Rev.	60.00
1861	Washington in center; seated figure at left. Blank Rev.	8.00
1861	Female and money chests; two sailors at left. Blank Rev.	3.00

Year	Portrait or Main Design	Used
1861	Railroad train; female with anchor at left; female with scales at right. Blank Rev.	225.00
1861	Jefferson Davis. Blank Rev.	6.00
1862	Jefferson Davis. Green Rev.	5.00
1863	Similar to above except for date.	5.00
1864	Similar to above except for date and a Blue Rev.	2.00

100 DOLLAR NOTES

1861	Railroad train in center; Liberty at left. Blank Rev. Montgomery, Ala.	700.00
1861	Railroad train in center; Justice at left; Minerva at right. Blank Rev.	65.00
1861	Two females in cloud; Washington at left. Blank Rev.	50.00
1861	Negroes loading cotton wagon; sailor at left. Blank Rev.	3.00
1862	Railroad train; milkmaid at left. Blank Rev.	2.00
1862	Negroes in cotton field; J. C. Calhoun at left; Liberty at right. Blank Rev.	3.00
1862	Lucy Pickens; two soldiers at left; Randolph at right. Green Rev.	17.50
1863	Similar to above except for date.	5.50
1864	Similar to above except for date and a Blue Rev.	1.50

500 DOLLAR NOTES

1861	Train on bridge; cattle below. Blank Rev. Montgomery, Ala.	1,750.00
1864	Confederate flag over horseman at left; "Stonewall" Jackson at right. Blank Rev.	20.00

1000 DOLLAR NOTE

1861	John C. Calhoun and Andrew Jackson. Blank Rev. Montgomery, Ala.	1,950.00

CONFEDERATE COIN ISSUES

No Confederate coin was ever struck for actual circulation. However, four genuine trial specimens of a half dollar were allegedly struck. The reverse die of this coin was used at a later date to manufacture restrikes and it is these restrikes which appear on the market. Genuine U.S. half dollars of 1861 were used for this purpose, the reverse being planed off and then struck with the Confederate die.

The so-called Confederate Cent of 1861 shows a Liberty Head on the Obv. and the value on the Rev. A few specimens were struck privately in Philadelphia at the instigation of the Confederacy, but no coins were ever delivered. Both restrikes and modern replicas exist of this coin.

CONFEDERATE SILVER HALF DOLLAR.	1861	Fine	300.00
CONFEDERATE COPPER CENT.	1861	Proof	800.00

THE COINAGE OF BRITISH NORTH AMERICA
Canada

LARGE CENTS
Head of Queen Victoria

Date	Amount Minted	Value	Date	Amount Minted	Value
1858	421,000	10.00	1892	1¼ million	.40
1859	9½ million	.30	1893	2 million	.30
1876-H	4 million	.30	1894	1 million	1.50
1881-H	2 million	.40	1895	1¼ million	.60
1882-H	4 million	.30	1896	2 million	.40
1884	2½ million	.30	1897	1½ million	.40
1886	1½ million	.65	1898-H	1 million	1.25
1887	1½ million	.65	1899	2½ million	.40
1888	4 million	.30	1900	1 million	1.25
1890-H	1 million	1.50	1900-H	2⅔ million	.30
1891 Large date	1½ million	1.50	1901	4 million	.30
1891 Small date	Part of above	12.50			

Head of King Edward VII

Date	Amount Minted	Value	Date	Amount Minted	Value
1902	3 million	.25	1907	2½ million	.25
1903	4 million	.25	1907-H	800,000	3.00
1904	2½ million	.30	1908	2⅓ million	.25
1905	2 million	.30	1909	4 million	.20
1906	4 million	.25	1910	5 million	.20

Head of King George V

Date	Amount Minted	Value	Date	Amount Minted	Value
1911	4⅔ million	.25	1916	11 million	.11
1912	5 million	.20	1917	12 million	.11
1913	5¾ million	.20	1918	13 million	.11
1914	3½ million	.20	1919	11¼ million	.11
1915	4¾ million	.20	1920	7 million	.11

SMALL CENTS

Head of King George V

Date	Amount Minted	Value	Date	Amount Minted	Value
1920	15½ million	.04	1925	1 million	3.50
1921	7½ million	.06	1926	2¼ million	.50
1922	1¼ million	4.00	1927	3½ million	.40
1923	1 million	7.00	1928	9 million	.03
1924	1½ million	2.00	1929	12¼ million	.03

Date	Amount Minted	Value	Date	Amount Minted	Value
1930	2½ million	.60	1934	7 million	.02
1931	3¾ million	.20	1935	7½ million	.02
1932	21⅓ million	.02	1936	8¾ million	.02
1933	12 million	.02			

Head of King George VI

(The following valuations are for coins in brilliant, new condition, and showing no
signs of wear. Used or circulated Cents from 1937 to date
do not command a premium.)

		NEW			NEW
1937	10 million	2.00	1946	56⅔ million	.25
1938	18⅓ million	1.00	1947	31 million	.70
1939	21⅔ million	1.00	1947 Maple leaf	43¾ million	.35
1940	85¾ million	.60	1948	24¾ million	.75
1941	56⅓ million	1.00	1949	33⅓ million	.25
1942	76 million	1.00	1950	60½ million	.25
1943	89 million	.60	1951	80½ million	.25
1944	44¼ million	1.00	1952	67⅔ million	.25
1945	77¼ million	.25			

Obv. Type	Rev. Type	Obv. Type	Commemorative
1953-1964	1937-	1965-	Rev. 1967

Head of Queen Elizabeth II
(The valuations are for coins in brilliant, new condition)

		NEW			NEW
1953	72¼ million	.25	1968	329⅔ million	.01
1954	22 million	.60	1969	335¼ million	.01
1955	56⅔ million	.20	1970	311¼ million	.01
1956	78⅔ million	.20	1971	298¼ million	.01
1957	100½ million	.20	1972	451⅓ million	.01
1958	57¾ million	.20	1973	457 million	.01
1959	83⅔ million	.05	1974	692 million	.01
1960	75¾ million	.05	1975	642⅓ million	.01
1961	139½ million	.05	1976	701 million	.01
1962	227¼ million	.05	1977	453 million	.01
1963	279 million	.05	1978	911 million	.01
1964	484⅔ million	.05	1979	754 million	.01
1965	304½ million	.01	1980	911¾ million	.01
1966	183⅔ million	.01	1981	1¼ billion	.01
1967	345¼ million	.01	1982		.01

SILVER 5 CENTS

Head of Queen Victoria

(The following valuations are for coins in G-VG condition)

Date	Amount Minted	Value	Date	Amount Minted	Value
1858 Small date	1½ million	3.50	1887	500,000	3.00
1858 Large date	Part of above	35.00	1888	1 million	1.10
1870	2¾ million	2.25	1889	1¼ million	4.50
1871	1½ million	2.25	1890-H	1 million	1.00
1872-H	2 million	1.75	1891	1¾ million	1.10
1874-H	800,000	2.25	1892	860,000	1.25
1875-H	1 million	20.00	1893	1¾ million	1.00
1880-H	3 million	.75	1894	500,000	3.75
1881-H	1½ million	1.25	1896	1½ million	1.00
1882-H	1 million	1.50	1897	1⅓ million	1.00
1883-H	600,000	2.50	1898	580,717	2.00
1884	200,000	17.50	1899	3 million	.75
1885	1 million	1.50	1900	1¾ million	.75
1886	1¾ million	1.10	1901	2 million	.75

Head of King Edward VII

Date	Amount Minted	Value	Date	Amount Minted	Value
1902	2 million	.50	1906	3 million	.60
1902-H	2¼ million	.50	1907	5¼ million	.45
1903	1 million	1.00	1908	1¼ million	1.50
1903-H	2⅔ million	.70	1909	1¾ million	.75
1904	2⅓ million	.70	1910	6 million	.55
1905	2⅔ million	.70			

Head of King George V

Date	Amount Minted	Value	Date	Amount Minted	Value
1911	3⅔ million	.60	1917	5⅔ million	.35
1912	5¾ million	.35	1918	5¾ million	.35
1913	5½ million	.35	1919	8 million	.35
1914	4¼ million	.35	1920	10⅔ million	.35
1915	1¼ million	1.50	1921	2½ million	600.00
1916	2⅓ million	.60			

NICKEL 5 CENTS

Head of King George V

Date	Amount Minted	Value	Date	Amount Minted	Value
1922	4¾ million	.06	1930	3⅔ million	.07
1923	2½ million	.07	1931	5 million	.06
1924	3 million	.06	1932	3¼ million	.07
1925	200,050	14.50	1933	2½ million	.07
1926	933,577	1.25	1934	3¾ million	.06
1927	5¼ million	.06	1935	3¾ million	.06
1928	4½ million	.06	1936	4⅓ million	.06
1929	5½ million	.06			

Beaver Type
1937-1942 & 1946-1952

V for Victory
1943-1945

Nickel
Bicentennial
1951

Head of King George VI

Beginning with the 1942 Tombac issue, the shape of the nickel is 12-sided, rather than round

Date	Amount Minted	Value	Date	Amount Minted	Value
1937	5 million	.05	1946	7 million	.05
1938	4 million	.05	1947	7⅔ million	.05
1939	5⅔ million	.05	1947 Maple Leaf	9½ million	.05
1940	14 million	.05	1948	1¾ million	.15
1941	8⅔ million	.05	1949	13 million	.05
1942-Nickel	6¾ million	.05	1950	12 million	.05
1942 Tombac	3⅓ million	.08	1951 Regular	4⅓ million	.05
1943	24¾ million	.05	1951 Commem.	9 million	.05
1944	11½ million	.05	1952	10¾ million	.05
1945	18¾ million	.05			

| 12-sided 1953-1962 | Mature Head Type | Commemorative |
| Round 1963-1964 | 1965- | Rev. 1967 |

Head of Queen Elizabeth II

		NEW			NEW
1953	16⅔	.75	1968	99¼ million	.05
1954	7 million	.75	1969	27¾ million	.05
1955	5⅓ million	.50	1970	5¾ million	.05
1956	9⅓ million	.25	1971	27⅓ million	.05
1957	7⅓ million	.25	1972	62½ million	.05
1958	7½ million	.25	1973	53½ million	.05
1959	11½ million	.10	1974	94¾ million	.05
1960	37 million	.07	1975	138⁴/₅ million	.05
1961	47¾ million	.06	1976	55 million	.05
1962	46¼ million	.06	1977	89 million	.05
1963	44 million	.06	1978	137 million	.05
1964	78 million	.05	1979	186¼ million	.05
1965	84¾ million	.05	1980	134¾ million	.05
1966	27½ million	.05	1981	99 million	.05
1967	58¾ million	.05	1982		.05

10 CENTS

Head of Queen Victoria

1858	1¼ million	3.00	1880-H	1½ million	2.25
1870	1⅔ million	2.75	1881-H	950,000	3.25
1871	800,000	3.00	1882-H	1 million	1.75
1871-H	1¾ million	4.75	1883-H	300,000	4.50
1872-H	1 million	20.00	1884	150,000	20.00
1874-H	600,000	2.25	1885	400,000	3.25
1875-H	1 million	40.00	1886	800,000	3.00

Date	Amount Minted	Value	Date	Amount Minted	Value
1887	350,000	2.75	1893 Round top 3. Part of above		175.00
1888	500,000	2.75	1894	500,000	1.75
1889	600,000	120.00	1896	650,000	1.25
1890-H	450,000	2.75	1898	720,000	1.25
1891	800,000	2.75	1899	1¼ million	.75
1892	520,000	2.25	1900	1 million	.50
1893 Flat top 3	500,000	2.25	1901	1¼ million	.50

Head of King Edward VII

Date	Amount Minted	Value	Date	Amount Minted	Value
1902	720,000	.50	1906	1⅔ million	.50
1902-H	1 million	.50	1907	2⅔ million	.50
1903	500,000	.75	1908	761,631	.50
1903-H	1⅓ million	.50	1909	1½ million	.50
1904	1 million	.75	1910	4⅔ million	.50
1905	1 million	.65			

Head of King George V

Date	Amount Minted	Value	Date	Amount Minted	Value
1911	2¾ million	2.75	1921	2½ million	.50
1912	3¼ million	.50	1928	2½ million	.50
1913 Small leaves	3½ million	.50	1929	3¼ million	.50
1913 large leaves	Part of above	20.00	1930	1¾ million	.50
1914	2½ million	.50	1931	2 million	.50
1915	672,408	.50	1932	1¼ million	.50
1916	4¼ million	.50	1933	672,368	.50
1917	5 million	.50	1934	384,056	.50
1918	5 million	.50	1935	384,592	.50
1919	7¾ million	.50	1936	2¾ million	.50
1920	6¼ million	.50			

Head of King George VI

Date	Amount Minted	Value	Date	Amount Minted	Value
1937	2½ million	.50	1946	6⅓ million	.50
1938	4¼ million	.50	1947	4½ million	.50
1939	5½ million	.50	1947 Maple leaf 9⅔ million		.50
1940	16½ million	.50	1948	422,741	1.25
1941	8¾ million	.50	1949	11⅓ million	.50
1942	10¼ million	.50	1950	17¾ million	.50
1943	21¼ million	.50	1951	15 million	.50
1944	9⅓ million	.50	1952	10½ million	.50
1945	11 million	.50			

Obv. Type 1953-1964	Rev. Type 1937-	Obv. Type 1965-	Commemorative Rev. 1967

Head of Queen Elizabeth II

Date	Amount Minted	Value	Date		Amount Minted	Value
1953	18½ million	.50	1968	Silver	70½ million	.30
1954	4½ million	.50	1968	Nickel	107 million	.10
1955	12¼ million	.50	1969		55¾ million	.10
1956	16¾ million	.50	1970		5¼ million	.10
1957	15⅔ million	.50	1971		41 million	.10
1958	11 million	.50	1972		60 million	.10
1959	19⅔ million	.50	1973		167¾ million	.10
1960	45½ million	.50	1974		201½ million	.10
1961	26¾ million	.50	1975		207⅔ million	.10
1962	41¾ million	.50	1976		95 million	.10
1963	42 million	.50	1977		128½ million	.10
1964	49½ million	.50	1978		170⅓ million	.10
1965	57 million	.50	1979		237 million	.10
1966	34⅓ million	.50	1980		169¾ million	.10
1967	63 million	.50	1981		124 million	.10
			1982			.10

20 CENTS

Head of Queen Victoria

Date	Amount Minted	Value
1858	750,000	20.00

25 CENTS

Head of Queen Victoria

Date	Amount Minted	Value	Date	Amount Minted	Value
1870	900,000	3.75	1887	100,000	15.00
1871	400,000	4.50	1888	400,000	2.75
1871-H	748,000	4.50	1889	66,340	17.50
1872-H	2¼ million	3.25	1890-H	200,000	3.25
1874-H	1⅔ million	3.25	1891	120,000	7.00
1875-H	1 million	75.00	1892	510,000	2.75
1880-H	400,000	4.25	1893	100,000	7.00
1881-H	820,000	3.50	1894	220,000	2.75
1882-H	600,000	3.75	1899	415,580	2.50
1883-H	960,000	2.50	1900	1⅓ million	2.50
1885	192,000	17.50	1901	640,000	2.50
1886	540,000	2.75			

Head of King Edward VII

Date	Amount Minted	Value	Date	Amount Minted	Value
1902	464,000	1.75	1906	1¼ million	1.75
1902-H	800,000	1.75	1907	2 million	1.75
1903	846,150	1.75	1908	466,625	1.75
1904	400,000	1.75	1909	1⅓ million	1.75
1905	800,000	1.75	1910	3½ million	1.75

Head of King George V

Date	Amount Minted	Value	Date	Amount Minted	Value
1911	1⅔ million	3.75	1927	468,096	2.00
1912	2½ million	1.75	1928	2 million	1.75
1913	2¼ million	1.75	1929	2⅔ million	1.75
1914	1¼ million	1.75	1930	961,174	1.75
1915	238,378	1.75	1931	537,815	1.75
1916	1½ million	1.75	1932	537,994	1.75
1917	3¼ million	1.75	1933	421,282	1.75
1918	4¼ million	1.75	1934	384,505	1.75
1919	5¾ million	1.75	1935	537,997	1.75
1920	2 million	1.75	1936	972,094	1.75
1921	575,268	2.50	1936 Dot below date	153,685	7.00

Head of King George VI

Date	Amount Minted	Value	Date	Amount Minted	Value
1937	2⅔ million	1.25	1946	2¼ million	1.25
1938	3¼ million	1.25	1947	1½ million	1.25
1939	3½ million	1.25	1947 Maple leaf	4⅓ million	1.25
1940	9½ million	1.25	1948	2½ million	1.25
1941	6⅔ million	1.25	1949	8 million	1.25
1942	7 million	1.25	1950	9⅔ million	1.25
1943	13½ million	1.25	1951	8¼ million	1.25
1944	7¼ million	1.25	1952	8¾ million	1.25
1945	5¼ million	1.25			

Obv. Type 1953-1964	Rev. Type 1937-	Obv. Type 1965-	Commemorative Rev. 1967	Commemorative Rev. 1973

Head of Queen Elizabeth II

Date	Amount Minted	Value	Date	Amount Minted	Value
1953	11¼ million	1.25	1960	22¾ million	1.25
1954	2⅓ million	1.25	1961	18¼ million	1.25
1955	9½ million	1.25	1962	29½ million	1.25
1956	11¼ million	1.25	1963	21¼ million	1.25
1957	12⅓ million	1.25	1964	36½ million	1.25
1958	9¾ million	1.25	1965	44¾ million	1.25
1959	13½ million	1.25	1966	25⅓ million	1.25

Date	Amount Minted	Value	Date	Amount Minted	Value
1967	48¾ million	1.25	1974	192⅓ million	.25
1968 Silver	71½ million	1.25	1975	141 million	.25
1968 Nickel	88⅔ million	.25	1976	86⁴/₅ million	.25
1969	133 million	.25	1977	99⅔ million	.25
1970	10⅓ million	.25	1978	176½ million	.25
1971	48 million	.25	1979	131 million	.25
1972	43¾ million	.25	1980	76 million	.25
1973	135 million	.25	1981	131½ million	.25
			1982		.25

50 CENTS

Head of Queen Victoria

Date	Amount Minted	Value	Date	Amount Minted	Value
1870	450,000	15.00	1892	151,000	7.50
1871	200,000	15.00	1894	29,036	60.00
1871-H	45,000	30.00	1898	100,000	7.50
1872-H	80,000	12.50	1899	50,000	22.50
1881-H	150,000	12.50	1900	118,000	12.50
1888	60,000	30.00	1901	80,000	12.50
1890-H	20,000	200.00			

Head of King Edward VII

Date	Amount Minted	Value	Date	Amount Minted	Value
1902	120,000	4.00	1907	300,000	4.25
1903-H	140,000	5.00	1908	121,260	4.25
1904	60,000	25.00	1909	198,648	4.25
1905	40,000	25.00	1910	640,141	4.25
1906	350,000	4.25			

The valuations listed in this book closely approximate how much established coin dealers will pay for any material needed in their stock.

Head of King George V

Date	Amount Minted	Value	Date	Amount Minted	Value
1911	204,475	**4.25**	1920	559,521	**4.50**
1912	283,248	**4.25**	1921	176,793	**2,500.00**
1913	263,290	**4.25**	1929	228,021	**4.25**
1914	157,537	**4.50**	1931	57,581	**4.25**
1916	454,853	**4.50**	1932	19,213	**20.00**
1917	739,715	**4.50**	1934	38,435	**4.25**
1918	832,805	**4.50**	1936	38,550	**4.25**
1919	1 million	**4.50**			

Head of King George VI

Date	Amount Minted	Value	Date	Amount Minted	Value
1937	192,016	**3.00**	1947	424,885	**2.50**
1938	192,018	**3.00**	1947 Maple leaf, straight 7.		
1939	287,976	**3.00**		38,433	**10.00**
1940	2 million	**3.00**	1947 Maple leaf, curved 7.		
1941	1⅔ million	**3.00**		Part of above.	**400.00**
1942	2 million	**3.00**	1948	37,784	**25.00**
1943	3 million	**3.00**	1949	858,991	**2.50**
1944	2½ million	**3.00**	1950	2⅓ million	**2.50**
1945	2 million	**3.00**	1951	2½ million	**2.50**
1946	950,235	**3.00**	1952	2½ million	**2.50**

**(The valuations in this book are based on the coins
being in G-VG condition, unless otherwise noted.)**

Obv. Type	First Rev. Type	Second Rev. Type	Commem.	Obv. Type
1953-1964	1953-1958	1959-	Rev. 1967	1965-

Head of Queen Elizabeth II

Date	Amount Minted	Value	Date	Amount Minted	Value
1953	1¾ million	2.50	1968	Nickel, reduced size, 4 mil.	.50
1954	506,305	2.50	1969	7⅓ million	.50
1955	753,511	2.50	1970	2½ million	.50
1956	1⅓ million	2.50	1971	2¼ million	.50
1957	2¼ million	2.50	1972	2½ million	.50
1958	3 million	2.50	1973	2½ million	.50
1959	3 million	2.50	1974	3½ million	.50
1960	3½ million	2.50	1975	3¾ million	.50
1961	3½ million	2.50	1976	3 million	.50
1962	5¼ million	2.50	1977	709,939	1.00
1963	8⅓ million	2.50	1978	3⅓ million	.50
1964	9⅓ million	2.50	1979	3½ million	.50
1965	12⅔ million	2.50	1980	1½ million	.50
1966	7⅔ million	2.50	1981	2¾ million	.50
1967	4¼ million	2.50	1982		.50

SILVER DOLLARS

Commemorative	Regular Issue	Rev. Type
1935	1936	1935-1936

Head of King George V

		Used	Unc			Used	Unc
1935	428,120	11.00	35.00	1936	306,100	11.00	35.00

Obv. Type
1937-1952

Regular Rev.
1937-1952

Commemorative Rev.
1939

Commemorative Rev.
1949

Head of King George VI

Date	Amount Minted	Used	Unc	Date	Amount Minted	Used	Unc
1937	241,002	11.00	35.00	1947 Maple			
1938	90,304	15.00	100.00	leaf	21,135	70.00	350.00
1939	1⅓ million	7.50	14.00	1948	18,780	500.00	1,000.00
1945	38,391	50.00	300.00	1949	672,298	12.50	25.00
1946	93,055	17.50	80.00	1950	261,002	12.50	20.00
1947 Blunt 7	65,595	30.00	100.00	1951	420,620	9.00	15.00
1947 Pointed 7				1952	408,835	9.00	15.00
	Part of above	75.00	400.00				

Obv. Type
1953-1964

Regular Rev. Type

Obv. Type
1965-

Commemorative Rev.
1958

Commemorative Rev.
1964

Commemorative Rev.
1967

Commemorative Rev.
1970

Commemorative Rev.
Nickel—1971

Commemorative Rev.
Silver—1971

Commemorative Rev.
Nickel—1973

Commemorative Rev.
Silver—1973

Commemorative Rev.
1974

Commemorative Rev.
Silver—1975

Commemorative Rev.
Silver—1976

Commemorative Rev.
Silver—1977

Head of Queen Elizabeth II

Date	Amount Minted	Used	Unc	Date	Amount Minted	Used	Unc
1953	1 million	7.50	9.00	1974 Nickel 2¾ million			1.00
1954	242,815	7.50	9.00	1974 Silver, proof-like, cased,			
1955	274,810	7.50	9.00		977,644		5.00
1956	209,092	7.50	9.00	1975 Nickel 3¼ million			1.00
1957	496,389	7.50	9.00	1975 Silver, proof-like, cased			
1958	3 million	7.50	9.00		931,000		5.00
1959	1½ million	7.50	9.00	1976 Nickel 2½ million			1.00
1960	1½ million	7.50	9.00	1976 Silver, proof-like cased,			
1961	1¼ million	7.50	9.00		483,722		5.00
1962	1¾ million	7.50	9.00	1977 Nickel 1⅓ million			1.00
1963	4¼ million	7.50	9.00	1977 Silver, proof-like, cased,			
1964	7¼ million	7.50	9.00		744,848		5.00
1965	10¾ million	7.50	9.00	1978 Nickel 3 million			1.00
1966	10 million	7.50	9.00	1978 Silver, proof-like, cased,			
1967	7 million	7.50	9.00		709,602		5.00
1968 Nickel, reduced size, 6 mil.			1.00	1979 Nickel 2½ million			1.00
1969	4¾ million		1.00	1979 Silver, proof-like, cased,			
1970	4¼ million		1.00		826,695		5.00
1971 Nickel 4¼ million			1.00	1980 Nickel			1.00
1971 Silver, proof-like, cased,				1980 Silver, proof-like, cased			10.00
	555,564		5.00	1981 Nickel			1.00
1972 Nickel 2⅖ million			1.00	1981 Silver, proof-like, cased			10.00
1972 Silver, proof-like, cased,				1982 Nickel			1.00
	350,019		5.00	1982 Silver, proof-like, cased			9.00
1973 Nickel 3¼ million			1.00				
1973 Silver, proof-like, cased,							
	709,670		5.00				

Olympic Commemorative Coins

The same obverse, the head of Queen Elizabeth II, appears on all of the coins. The valuations are for coins in brilliant, new condition.

SERIES 1, 1973

Denomination	Date	Reverse Design	Value
5 Dollars	1973	Map of North America	6.00
5 Dollars	1973	Kingston Skyline	6.00
10 Dollars	1973	Map of the World	12.00
10 Dollars	1973	Montreal Skyline	12.00
4-piece Uncirculated Set, cased			36.00
4-piece Proof Set, cased			45.00

SERIES II, 1974

5 Dollars	1974	Athlete with Olympic Torch	6.00
5 Dollars	1974	The Laurel Wreath	6.00
10 Dollars	1974	The Greek God, Zeus	12.00
10 Dollars	1974	The Temple of Zeus	12.00
4-piece Uncirculated Set, cased			36.00
4-piece Proof Set, cased			45.00

SERIES III, 1974

Denomination	Date	Reverse Design	Value
5 Dollars	1974	Canoeing	6.00
5 Dollars	1974	Rowing	6.00
10 Dollars	1974	Cyclists	12.00
10 Dollars	1974	Lacrosse	12.00
4-piece Uncirculated Set, cased			36.00
4-piece Proof Set, cased			45.00

SERIES IV, 1975

5 Dollars	1975	Marathon	6.00
5 Dollars	1975	Javelin	6.00
10 Dollars	1975	Hurdles	12.00
10 Dollars	1975	Shotput	12.00
4-piece Uncirculated Set, cased			36.00
4-piece Proof Set, cased			45.00

SERIES V, 1975

5 dollars	1975	Swimming	6.00
5 Dollars	1975	Diving	6.00
10 Dollars	1975	Sailing	12.00
10 Dollars	1975	Kayak	12.00
4-piece Uncirculated Set, cased			36.00
4-piece Proof Set, cased			45.00

SERIES VI, 1976

5 Dollars	1976	Fencing	6.00
5 Dollars	1976	Boxing	6.00
10 Dollars	1976	Soccer	12.00
10 Dollars	1976	Field hockey	12.00
4-piece Uncirculated Set, cased			36.00
4-piece Proof Set, cased			45.00

SERIES VII, 1976

5 Dollars	1976	Olympic Village	6.00
5 Dollars	1976	Olympic Flame	6.00
10 Dollars	1976	Olympic Stadium	12.00
10 Dollars	1976	Olympic Velodrome	12.00
4-piece Uncirculated Set, cased			36.00
4-piece Proof Set, cased			45.00

GOLD COINS

Canadian Types

Head of King George V

5 DOLLARS

Date	Amount Minted	Value
1912	165,680	150.00
1913	98,832	150.00
1914	31,122	450.00

10 DOLLARS

1912	74,759	400.00
1913	149,232	400.00
1914	140,068	400.00

Head of Queen Elizabeth II

20 DOLLARS

1967	337,512 proofs		250.00

50 DOLLARS

Maple Leaf Gold Bullion Coins

1979	1 million	550.00
1980		550.00

100 DOLLARS

1976 27 mm. Olympics (.585)			
	572,387		100.00
1976 25 mm. Olympics			
	335,779	proofs	250.00
1977 Jubilee	180,396	proofs	250.00
1978 Geese	200,000	proofs	250.00
1979 Children	250,000	proofs	250.00
1980 Eskimo	300,000	proofs	250.00
1981 National Anthem			
	102,000	proofs	250.00
1982 Constitution		proofs	200.00

English Type Sovereigns or Pounds

Normal type Gold 1 Pound pieces of English design, struck at the Ottawa Mint and with the "C" mint mark on the ground under the horse. The coins from 1908 through 1910 are with the head of Edward VII and those from 1911 through 1919 are with the head of George V.

1 Pound 1908-C	636	900.00	1 Pound 1914-C	14,891	175.00
1 Pound 1909-C	16,273	200.00	1 Pound 1916-C	6,111	Rare
1 Pound 1910-C	28,012	180.00	1 Pound 1917-C	58,845	150.00
1 Pound 1911-C	256,946	150.00	1 Pound 1918-C	106,516	150.00
1 Pound 1913-C	3,715	475.00	1 Pound 1919-C	135,889	150.00

Newfoundland

LARGE CENTS

Head of Queen Victoria

Date	Amount Minted	Value	Date	Amount Minted	Value
1865	240,000	.30	1885	40,000	**4.50**
1872-H	200,000	.30	1888	50,000	**3.75**
1873	200,025	.30	1890	200,000	.30
1876-H	200,000	.30	1894	200,000	.30
1880	400,000	.30	1896	200,000	.30

Head of King Edward VII

Date	Amount Minted	Value	Date	Amount Minted	Value
1904-H	100,000	.75	1909	200,000	.30
1907	200,000	.30			

Head of King George V

Date	Amount Minted	Value	Date	Amount Minted	Value
1913	400,000	.15	1920-C	302,184	.15
1917-C	702,350	.15	1929	300,000	.15
1919-C	300,000	.15	1936	300,000	.15

SMALL CENTS

Head of King George VI

Date	Amount Minted	Value	Date	Amount Minted	Value
1938	500,000	.10	1943-C	1¼ million	.10
1940	300,000	.40	1944-C	1⅓ million	.10
1941-C	827,662	.10	1947-C	313,772	.10
1942	2 million	.10			

SILVER 5 CENTS

Head of Queen Victoria

Date	Amount Minted	Value	Date	Amount Minted	Value
1865	80,000	6.00	1881	40,000	3.75
1870	40,000	6.50	1882-H	60,000	3.00
1872-H	40,000	6.00	1885	16,000	20.00
1873	44,260	6.50	1888	40,000	3.75
1873-H	Part of above	100.00	1890	160,000	1.00
1876-H	20,000	10.00	1894	160,000	1.00
1880	40,000	6.50	1896	400,000	.75

Head of King Edward VII

Date	Amount Minted	Value	Date	Amount Minted	Value
1903	100,000	.50	1908	400,000	.50
1904-H	100,000	.50			

Head of King George V

Date	Amount Minted	Value	Date	Amount Minted	Value
1912	300,000	.50	1919-C	100,844	.50
1917-C	300,319	.50	1929	300,000	.50

Head of King George VI

Date	Amount Minted	Value	Date	Amount Minted	Value
1936	100,000	.30	1941-C	612,641	.30
1940-C	200,000	.30	1942-C	298,348	.50

Date	Amount Minted	Value	Date	Amount Minted	Value
1943-C	351,666	.30	1946-C	2,041	75.00
1944-C	286,504	.30	1947-C	38,400	.50
1945-C	203,828	.30			

10 CENTS

Head of Queen Victoria

Date	Amount Minted	Value	Date	Amount Minted	Value
1865	80,000	2.75	1882-H	20,000	1.50
1870	30,000	25.00	1885	8,000	11.00
1872-H	40,000	2.25	1888	30,000	1.75
1873	23,614	3.00	1890	100,000	.75
1876-H	10,000	5.50	1894	100,000	.75
1880	10,000	5.50	1896	230,000	.60

Head of King Edward VII

Date	Amount Minted	Value	Date	Amount Minted	Value
1903	100,000	.60	1904-H	100,000	.60

Head of King George V

Date	Amount Minted	Value	Date	Amount Minted	Value
1912	150,000	.60	1919-C	54,342	60
1917-C	250,805	.60			

Head of King George VI

Date	Amount Minted	Value	Date	Amount Minted	Value
1938	100,000	.60	1944-C	151,471	.60
1940	100,000	.60	1945-C	175,833	.60
1941-C	483,630	.60	1946-C	38,400	1.25
1942-C	292,736	.60	1947-C	61,988	.60
1943-C	104,706	.60			

20 CENTS

Head of Queen Victoria

Date	Amount Minted	Value	Date	Amount Minted	Value
1865	100,000	1.25	1885	40,000	1.25
1870	50,000	1.75	1888	75,000	1.25
1872-H	90,000	1.25	1890	100,000	1.25
1873	45,797	1.50	1894	100,000	1.25
1876-H	50,000	1.50	1896	125,000	1.25
1880	30,000	1.50	1899	125,000	1.25
1881	60,000	1.25	1900	125,000	1.25
1882-H	100,000	1.25			

Head of King Edward VII

Date	Amount Minted	Value
1904-H	75,000	1.50

Head of King George V

Date	Amount Minted	Value	Date	Amount Minted	Value
1912	350,000	**1.25**			

25 CENTS

Head of King George V

Date	Amount Minted	Value	Date	Amount Minted	Value
1917-C	464,779	**1.50**	1919-C	163,939	**1.50**

50 CENTS

Head of Queen Victoria

Date	Amount Minted	Value	Date	Amount Minted	Value
1870	50,000	**3.00**	1885	40,000	**3.00**
1872-H	48,000	**3.00**	1888	20,000	**3.00**
1873	37,675	**3.00**	1894	40,000	**3.00**
1874	80,000	**3.00**	1896	60,000	**3.00**
1876-H	28,000	**4.00**	1898	76,607	**3.00**
1880	24,000	**4.00**	1899	150,000	**3.00**
1881	50,000	**3.00**	1900	150,000	**3.00**
1882-H	100,000	**3.00**			

Head of King Edward VII

Date	Amount Minted	Value	Date	Amount Minted	Value
1904-H	140,000	**3.00**	1908	160,000	**3.00**
1907	100,000	**3.00**	1909	200,000	**3.00**

Head of King George V

1911	200,000	**3.00**	1918-C	294,824	**3.00**
1917-C	375,560	**3.00**	1919-C	306,267	**3.00**

GOLD COINS

2 DOLLARS

Head of Queen Victoria

1865	10,000	**140.00**	1881	10,000	**140.00**
1870	10,000	**140.00**	1882-H	25,000	**140.00**
1872	6,050	**200.00**	1885	10,000	**140.00**
1880	2,500	**500.00**	1888	25,000	**140.00**

New Brunswick

(*All coins are with the head of Queen Victoria*)

Coin	Date	Amount Minted	Value
Half Cent	1861	222,800	15.00
Large Cent	1861	1 million	.25
Large Cent	1864	1 million	.25
Silver 5 Cents	1862	100,000	10.00
Silver 5 Cents	1864	100,000	10.00
10 Cents	1862	150,000	7.50
10 Cents	1864	100,000	7.50
20 Cents	1862	150,000	4.00
20 Cents	1864	150,000	4.00

Nova Scotia

(*All coins are with the head of Queen Victoria*)

Coin	Date	Amount Minted	Value
Half Cent	1861	460,000	1.25
Half Cent	1864	400,000	1.25
Large Cent	1861	800,000	.25
Large Cent	1862	100,000	3.50
Large Cent	1864	800,000	.25

Prince Edward Island

(Head of Queen Victoria)

Coin	Date	Amount Minted	Value
Large Cent	1871	1 million	.25

British Columbia

Very rare gold coins that were not placed in circulation

| 10 Dollars | 1862 | —— |
| 20 Dollars | 1862 | —— |

(The valuations in this book are based on the coins being in G-VG condition, unless otherwise noted.)